EARN MONEY IN YOUR TEEN BUSINESS

Proven, Practical Strategies for Teen Entrepreneurship and Step by Step Guidance to Create Monthly Cash Flow and Independent Income

Best Selling Teen Money Series

Book 1

CHRIS ROSENBERG

To my husband Mike, our two boys, Nate and J, and to our family, who loves and lives in the spirit of entrepreneurship, learning, growth and ongoing daily adventures.

Contents

PHASE THREE SCALE:

Introduction

Entrepreneurialism levels the playing field. What matters is your mindset and your ability to execute. Everything else is picked up along the way... It's one of the last remaining fields where you still get to earn income while developing your craft.

Meet Ryan. At 16, he started a small lawn care business in his neighborhood. It wasn't glamorous. It wasn't high-tech. But by the end of his first summer, Ryan had made over $5,000. He used that money to buy better equipment and expand his services. By his senior year, he was earning more than many adults. Ryan didn't have a huge budget or tons of experience. What he did have was determination and a willingness to learn on the go.

I'm Chris Rosenberg, and I've spent 25 years helping people achieve financial success. I've managed the wealth of self-made millionaires and scaled startups to eight-figure revenues. I've coached entrepreneurs at every level in between. I've also guided my own kids, ages 17 and 12, to develop and monetize multiple businesses. Now, I want to share these tools and strategies with you. All I expect in return is that you execute.

The purpose of this book is simple: to give you a step-by-step guide to start your own business and earn money now. We'll cover practical, actionable strategies that you can implement immediately. You don't need any amount of money, experience, or even have any idea where to start. All you do need is the desire and commitment to execute - this book will guide you every step of the way. And if you already have a business earning you money, we'll walk you through the steps you need to hit any revenue goal you desire.

Starting a business as a teen might seem like an enormous project, but the steps come together much quicker than you would think, and it gives you a huge advantage. You learn how to manage money, solve problems, and make decisions. Some say these skills are learned in school, but the difference is that you get to actually practice these skills in situations where they matter, not in theory like in other areas of your life. And the difference is astounding. Developing these skills will set you apart whether you decide to run your own business or work for someone else in the future. The headstart you get financially by starting as a teen sets you miles ahead of everyone else. You can earn enough to pay for college, buy a car or a house, or set yourself up for future wealth. The possibilities are endless - but the key is to start now.

Age doesn't matter. You can start where you are. Let's say you're really good in Math or English; it comes easy to you, you enjoy it, and you start a tutoring business and help dozens of students while making a profit. We'll walk through the steps to set the business up, ensure your profitability, get your first client, and then grow that business to hit your desired income goal. Countless adults have used these exact strategies to create six-figure businesses. The principles are the same, regardless of your age.

Entrepreneurial skills are invaluable. They teach you how to think critically, manage your time, and communicate effectively. These are skills that will benefit you in any career path you choose. Whether you become a small business owner or an employee on an amazing career path of your dreams, these skills will give you an incredible advantage, which translates directly into dollars.

But recognize - this book isn't just about knowledge. It's about execution. Lots of people know what to do, but very few actually do it. Information is only powerful when you take action. This book is designed to help you take that action step by step.

This book is for advanced teens like you. You wouldn't have picked up this book if you weren't ready to start something big. Whether you're just starting or have already earned income in multiple businesses, this book meets you where you are and takes you step-by-step to the next level of where you want to go. Everything is broken down into simple steps so you can act quickly and consistently.

Mixed into the chapters are references to other teen business owners. Many times, when you're exceptional, regardless of whether you're a teen or an adult, it can feel like there's literally no one like you. There are more successful teen business owners today than ever, especially in our global and digital world. Inserting their stories throughout the chapters is purposeful, as these are a handful of the countless success stories. A successful, cash-flowing teen business isn't just possible - it's more common now than ever. And the action that you're taking right now allows you to become the next teen success story to inspire the teens that come after you.

Every teen is different. Know your strengths and work with your parents in a way that sets you up for success. But remember, you learn by doing. Don't be surprised if your parents want to steal this book to start their own business. Let them - have it be like a family contest. Each of you start and grow your own independent business. The keys to launching a new independent income stream are all laid out here.

How should you use this book? Do not read it cover to cover. This book is a guide to walk you through taking action. Read, execute, read, execute. Don't move forward without taking action. Follow this step-by-step guide based on your specific Phase: Launch (earn your first dollars), Stabilize (earn consistent dollars), Scale (grow your dollars).

Here's what you can expect in this book. We'll start with developing the right mindset and setting goals. You can't get anywhere until you know where you want to go - then, you can craft a step-by-step roadmap to get there. Then, we'll move on to choosing the right business by monetizing your existing skills and leveraging your strengths. We'll walk you through the quickest way to get your first customer so you can start earning dollars. Then, we'll walk through how to grow your marketing, sales, and service to make sure you're earning more consistent dollars and hitting your revenue goals. Lastly, we'll explain how to scale your business to hit whatever revenue goals you desire, hire help so you can handle the increased customers you have, and which moves to start making now to set up your financial future. Remember - this isn't a book to read in one sitting. It's a book meant to be an action plan for your execution in various growth stages of your cash-flowing business. Just focus on the step you're currently on - execute and move to the next.

One of the most incredible advantages you have right now is time. Small financial moves now make millions later. But the question is—how do you make small financial moves now—where do you get the dollars? Enter your cash-flowing business. First, we teach you how to create dollars with a business, and then we can start the conversation about how to leverage those dollars to secure your financial future.

Each section will end with key takeaways and action steps. These steps will help you implement what you've learned and move forward. This book is designed to be actionable. It's about doing, not just reading.

This book offers everything you need to create a successful business and earn money now. It's time to take action. The path begins here, and the results can be life-changing. You've got to go through the steps, but the rewards are better than you can ever imagine.

Let's get started.

FOUNDATION

"EVERY STRUCTURE RISES AND FALLS ON
THE STRENGTH OF ITS FOUNDATION"

ONE

Mindset is the Make or Break

At just 12 years old, Noa Mintz started a nanny agency called Nannies by Noa. Armed with determination and a vision, she managed to grow her business to handle over 190 clients. What set her apart wasn't just her business idea but her mindset. She believed in her ability to succeed and didn't let anything hold her back. This Chapter is all about harnessing that same mindset because the truth of the matter is that your mindset will make or break your success.

Your Life 2.0

So, how do you actually hit your income goals? It starts with creating your new reality now, getting really clear about how much you want to make and what your life will look like on a day-to-day basis at that income level.

Be specific about what you want to achieve. Maybe it's earning enough to save for college, buying a car, or being able to travel anywhere you want in the world while being able to work and afford that lifestyle. The key is to set specific income targets. These targets give you something to aim for and make your goals real and achievable.

Next, really think about what your life is like at that income level. Let's say you want to make $2,500 a month - what will your day-to-day life look like? How does the 2.0 version of you, who is actually earning $2,500 a month, live? What does a day in the life look like? Are you waking up early and going to the gym? Do you block out specific times in the afternoon to manage and run your business? Do you meditate in the morning? Are you listening to an audiobook while doing laundry and stuff around the house? Think about the traits and behaviors of someone who has achieved your financial goals.

Successful business owners have routines that set them up for success. They start their day with a purpose. Some wake up early, exercise, and plan their day. They focus on tasks that drive their business forward and prioritize them. They manage their time effectively, balancing work, learning, and personal life. Start integrating these habits into your current life. Wake up a little earlier, set goals for the day, and prioritize your tasks. Small changes can lead to significant results. First you start living your life today like that $2,500 a month income earner - the money comes, not the other way around.

It's the same for any exceptional goal. Exceptional people make exceptional choices to create exceptional lives and get exceptional results. To achieve what others haven't, you must be willing to do what others won't.

KEY POINTS:

- The mindset always precedes the money.
- Mindset is the make or break for success in your business.

ACTION STEPS:

- Take a few minutes to write down your financial goals. Be specific. How much do you want to earn in the next month, six months, and year?
- Describe your 2.0 life and identify one habit you can start incorporating into your routine today. Maybe it's waking up 30 minutes earlier or setting daily goals. Start small and build from there.

In the next sections, we'll walk through all the steps you need to earn your first dollars and grow your business. But remember - first, the mindset, then the money.

How To "Crush It" At Life

Success isn't just about working hard; it's about working smart. Everyone's ideal schedule looks different, and it's key to know your strengths and where you would benefit from support to design a schedule that aligns with your life. Balancing a business with school, activities, and family life, as well as maintaining your physical and mental health, can seem like a tremendous amount to manage.

But there is a method to the madness. It's rarely about just trying harder or working more. If you're challenged by something, it's more likely that you need to change your strategy to play to your strengths in a different way to overcome the challenge and move forward. But we will cover that in more detail as we go on. Let's break it down with specific ways to help you manage everything effectively.

A solid morning routine can set the tone for your entire day. Tony Robbins starts his day with a cold plunge to reset his body and mind, while Maria Konnikova uses yoga and meditation to set a positive tone. These routines are not just habits; they are rituals that prepare them for a productive day. The benefits of a morning routine are invaluable. Every single successful person has developed some form of a morning routine. It helps you start your day with intention, increases productivity, and boosts your mood. When you're happy and you feel good - you accomplish more. Everything just works better. Here are three simple morning routines to consider:

1. The Early Bird Routine: Wake up at 5:00 a.m., do a 30-minute workout, eat a healthy breakfast, and review your goals for the day. This routine is excellent for those who thrive on having a head start.
2. The Mindful Morning: Wake up at 6:00 a.m., spend 15 minutes meditating, drink a glass of water, and read a book for 20 minutes. This routine helps reduce stress and improve focus.
3. The Balanced Start: Wake up at 6:30 a.m., do a quick 10-minute stretch, eat a nutritious breakfast, and spend 15 minutes planning your day. This routine is ideal for those who need a balanced approach to start their day.

Designing your own morning routine is about recognizing what energizes you and sets a positive tone for your day. Start by identifying activities that make you feel good and focused. Experiment with different routines until you find one that works best for you. Remember, the goal is to create a routine that prepares you mentally and physically for the day's challenges to set you up for success.

When you're adding another element, like starting a business, to the other elements you already have in your life - school, family, friends, sports, extracurriculars - learning how to manage your time so you don't lose your mind is critical. Many adults have yet to learn this skill. Time blocking is an underrated tool that is life changing. Sit down, open your Google calendar, and let's walk through setting it up together. First, start with the major parts of your week that are already scheduled, such as school, activities you're already committed to, etc. Those schedules are usually already fixed every week. Now, make a list of the remaining things that you want to accomplish every week in your 2.0 life that you get to schedule yourself.

Your overall schedule includes studying, working on your business, moving your body, hanging out with your friends, etc. Look at your calendar and map out weekly recurring calendar events for each of these priorities. When you schedule blocks of time to work on these various areas in your life and actually follow through on your schedule, all of a sudden, the amount of work you get done skyrockets. Now - this schedule isn't meant to be permanent. Make the schedule, stick to it for a week or so, and then adjust it to maximize its effectiveness for you and what you want to accomplish. The key is to learn what works for you and to achieve your goal by playing to your strengths.

Balancing time between business and personal life is a skill you'll develop as you go. It's easy to get caught up in work and neglect other areas of your life. But remember, maintaining a balance is key to long-term success. Make sure you allocate time for your mental and physical health, the things you enjoy, and spending time with family and friends. This balance will help you stay motivated and actually increase your effectiveness over time.

KEY POINTS:

- If you're struggling, stop pushing. Step back and change the strategy. Setting yourself up for success is about creating a schedule that works for you.
- Start your day with a solid morning routine.
- Use time blocking to manage your tasks and ensure you balance work with your personal life.

ACTION STEPS:

- Create the best morning routine for you and add it to your Google calendar.
- Set up your time-blocking schedule. List all your tasks, allocate specific time blocks for each activity, and add them to your Google calendar.
- Play it out through your week, and then review and adjust your schedule to find what works best for you.

The Mental Game

An unbreakable mindset can be the difference between success and failure. Rachel Zietz founded Gladiator Lacrosse at age 13. Rachel identified a gap in the market for durable and affordable lacrosse equipment. She faced skepticism and doubt, not just because of her age but also because she was entering a male-dominated industry. However, Rachel's mindset was focused solely on innovation and persistence. She focused on improving her products and succeeding regardless of what anyone else thought or said. Within two years, her company was valued at over $1 million. Rachel's story illustrates that with the right mindset, you can turn obstacles into opportunities and achieve incredible success (Source 2).

The difference between success and failure as a business owner often comes down to mindset. The actual steps to launch and grow a business aren't complicated. What trips most people up is their belief—or lack thereof—in themselves and their own personal ability to succeed. People fail because they don't believe in their potential or the achievability of their goals. The ones who make it are those who have their mental game on point. They show up and put in the effort, even when the going gets tough because they see what others don't: their inevitable success.

To accomplish what others haven't, you must be willing to do what others won't. This means embracing challenges, learning from failures, and continuously seeking opportunities to improve. So, how can you develop a growth mindset? Start by prioritizing continuous learning in your life, like you are right now, by reading this book. Exceptional people prioritize their own development, both mentally and physically. When you're working out and you hit a plateau, you level up so you're challenged again, and you can grow to the next level, right? The same principles apply to your mindset and your personal development. Start implementing and view challenges in your life and your business as opportunities to grow. Set incremental goals that are uncomfortable for you and cause you to stretch and grow outside your comfort zone but are achievable with effort. These are the steps to develop a mindset that sees potential in every situation.

Creating a business as a teen comes with immense benefits. Depending on your age, some steps require parental involvement, like setting up a bank account or signing contracts, but 99% of the tasks you can handle independently. Starting now allows you to earn cash flow and grow, providing financial benefits that will last for years. Even small financial steps now can lead to significant gains in the future. For example, a teenager who sets aside $100 a month can turn it into seven figures over time through smart investing and compounding interest. Take action to build a business that generates cash flow and sets you up for long-term financial success. The question everyone asks is always, where do you get the dollars to set aside so you can start building wealth? That's why we start by building a business to set you up with a stream to provide those dollars so you learn to grow those dollars for your future. We're going to walk through the steps to set you up for your financial success, but first, you have to start by earning those dollars to have them to set aside for your financial future.

KEY POINTS:

- Your mental game is the ultimate factor in your success as a business owner.
- Embrace challenges, and continuously seek goals that cause you to stretch and grow.
- Starting your business now creates invaluable opportunities to set you up for your financial future.
- Your 2.0 life is ready to start now.

TWO

Building Your 2.0 Life

I magine you're 15 years old, and you've just started a small business selling custom-designed phone cases. Your designs are amazing, and your friends love them. You decide to take it a step further and sell them online. Within months, you're overwhelmed with orders, and your business is booming. But then, a problem arises. Your supplier messes up a shipment, and you can't fulfill your orders on time. Customers start to complain, and your reputation is on the line. What do you do? This is where your word comes into play. How you handle this situation can make or break your business.

Do What You Say You're Going To Do

In the world of business, your word is everything. When you make a commitment to a customer or an employee, you have to come through, no matter the circumstance, even when it's completely out of your hands.

When you stand behind your word, you build trust. Trust is like a bridge between you and your customers. If you say you'll deliver a product by a certain date, make sure you do it. It doesn't matter why there's a supply issue or who caused it - you committed to your customers, and now you have to manage the situation. If there's a problem, communicate honestly and work to fix it. This approach not only retains customers but also turns them into loyal advocates for your business. It's a small world, and word of mouth travels fast. A reputation for honesty can set you apart and attract more customers.

But it's not just about customers. Your word matters to your employees and to partners who refer their customers to your business, too. Being reliable and consistent builds a strong team. When your team knows they can count on you, they are more likely to be motivated and dedicated and to refer you to more clients. This creates a positive work environment where everyone strives for success. Leaders who keep their promises foster loyalty and respect, which are crucial for long-term business growth.

Most importantly, your success comes down to whether or not you keep your word to yourself. When you set a goal or make a commitment, follow through. This is exactly how self-discipline and confidence are built. It's easy to make excuses, but holding yourself accountable is what separates successful entrepreneurs from the rest. If you promise yourself to finish a project by the end of the week or to do your morning routine every day to set yourself up for success, do it. This habit of self-accountability will spill over into other areas of your life, making you more dependable and trustworthy. Does your 2.0 version of yourself, earning $2,500 a month, keep their word? You are that person today.

Kobe Bryant once shared an impactful story about personal discipline and commitment, explaining how he approached his workout routine and self-improvement. He mentioned that when he made a commitment or an agreement with himself, such as deciding to work out or practice at certain times, he never renegotiated these "contracts" with himself. This meant that no matter how tired he was or how he felt on a given day, he followed through on his plans without allowing any excuses. For Kobe, the key was consistency and discipline, and this mindset helped him achieve greatness. He believed that by keeping his word to himself, he built mental toughness, discipline, and an unbreakable work ethic.

Remember, your word is a reflection of your character. People notice when you keep your promises and when you don't. In business, integrity isn't just a nice-to-have; it's a must-have. Your actions teach people who you are. Then, people decide whether or not to do business with you based on who you've taught them you are through your actions. Character, Integrity, and Honesty are shown in everything you do, and people will choose you over the competition every time, when you teach them through your actions that you embody these characteristics. (Source 1).

Setting and Crushing Goals

Setting goals is like creating a roadmap for your business. Anyone who doesn't love setting goals - just hasn't learned how to do it right. It's about setting them right, crushing them, and enjoying the win. Then, you know when you set the next goal - how much fun it's going to be to crush it, no matter the challenges that arise. Cause that's just who you are - you crush goals.

An easy way to break it down is the SMART method. SMART stands for Specific, Measurable, Achievable, Relevant, and Time-bound. Suppose you run a business offering swim lessons, and you want to earn $500 more a month. You charge $150 a month per kid for group swim lessons. A SMART goal would be: "I gained four new clients within 30 days by going online and responding to 5 posts a day where parents were looking for swim lessons." This goal is specific (gain four new clients), measurable (you can count clients and post responses), achievable (if you put in the effort), relevant (it helps your revenue directly grow), and time-bound (30 days). Don't worry - we are going to walk you through every step of how to do this so you can earn your dollars in your chosen business. The goal is written from a perspective where you've already accomplished it. Every time you read that goal, you should smile and feel what it feels like to have accomplished it.

Teens are doing this every day across the world. Take a teen who sets a sales target for his pool cleaning business, aiming to secure five new clients in two weeks. He achieved this by going door-to-door in his neighborhood and offering special promotions. These examples show that with clear goals and consistent effort, you can achieve impressive results, and they will have a direct impact on your revenue now.

Setting goals, taking direct action, and crushing those goals is both simple and fun. Productivity is about focusing on activities that generate revenue, not just keeping busy. Imagine you spend hours designing a logo but neglect to market your services or secure any new customers. The logo might look great, but without actually gaining new customers who generate revenue, what difference does it make? Does a logo mean you have a business? No. Generating revenue means you have a business. Earning a profit and personal income means you have a business. Many adults still haven't learned this lesson. You start and grow a business to earn money for you and your family. Prioritize tasks that directly impact your revenue, like reaching out to potential customers. It's easy to get caught up in non-revenue activities, but always ask yourself, "Is this helping me make money?" If the answer is no, adjust how you spend your time for your business time block on your calendar.

Tracking and adjusting your goals is essential both personally and for your business. Book a weekly calendar block in your Google calendar to review your goals and progress and make adjustments as necessary. Everyone makes adjustments to their goals based on performance. Don't see adjustments as failures. They're part of the process. Set new milestones based on your achievements and recognize when it's time to pivot. If a strategy isn't working, you adjust the strategy, not the goal. Think of it this way. Let's say you set out to go to Disneyland for the day. You map the address in your app, and then, as you go along the road, you see a huge accident. Do you turn back and give up on spending the day at Disneyland? No, that sounds insane. No one would do that. You recalculate the route and adjust based on the new information, and you take another path to get to Disneyland. No one gives up on the destination when there's a roadblock. Adjust the path - not the destination.

It all starts with setting your first goal. Aim to make your first sale within a matter of weeks. Honestly, you can make your first sale within your first week - as long as you keep working through the book. We have created many businesses in our family. One of the most recent projects was a family business that was a true passion of my husband's, but we built it as a family. We decided to launch a meal delivery business, and we went from idea to first sale in 10 days flat. It doesn't take a huge amount of time to generate dollars. You just need to take specific and decisive, strategic action and keep following through. That same family business grew dramatically, and we crossed the six-figure mark in our first nine months. That business is still thriving and a wonderful source of income and joy for our family today. We literally followed the exact steps I'm covering here in this book. It all starts with your first goal and your first dollars earned. Don't worry about how you're going to do it... we'll cover every step together. First, set the goal, and then follow the process.

KEY POINTS:

- Setting and crushing goals is fun if you're doing it right.
- SMART goals are extremely helpful but stretch you out of your comfort zone to grow.
- When you hit a roadblock, adjust the path - not the destination.
- It doesn't take a huge amount of time or money to earn your first dollar.

ACTION STEPS:

- Open up a Google Doc and write out your first SMART goal in large letters, taking up the whole page. Tape it on the wall by your bed so it's the first thing you see when you wake up and the last thing you look at before you go to sleep, and smile every time you look at it.
- First Smart Goal Template

Keeping Each Other On Track

Imagine you've just set a goal to launch an event planning business in your community and want to get your first customer within 30 days. You're incredibly excited but also a bit overwhelmed. We'll walk you through every step. But the steps are just one piece of the puzzle. This is where an accountability partner (or group) comes in. Think about who can help keep you on track. It could be a friend, a classmate, a relative, a teacher, or even a sibling. If your parents decide to start their own business alongside you as a competition, as we discussed in the Introduction, your built-in accountability partner will be there. Accountability partners are invaluable in so many areas of your life - working out, training for sports, studying, the list goes on. Why does it work better? Because we tend to show up for someone else when we make a commitment to each other, even more than we show up for ourselves alone. Accountability partners check in on each other regularly, give progress updates, and give each other that extra push when you need it. The right partner needs to be just as excited and committed about growing their own business as you are about growing yours.

You help each other stay focused and motivated, ensuring that you follow through on your commitments. For example, consider a teen who started a web design service. She chose her best friend as her accountability partner, who also ran a small business. They held each other accountable by meeting weekly to discuss their goals, challenges, and successes. When one was having a rough week, and the other one crushed it - it helped her have faith that she could crush it next week, too. This partnership kept them both motivated and on track, leading to significant growth in their respective businesses. Accountability helps you maintain focus, keeps you motivated, and provides a sense of responsibility, knowing that someone else is counting on you to succeed. Many teens are tempted to partner with a friend to start their new business. Don't do that. You and your friend need to each set up your own businesses and be accountability partners. It's 1,000 times more beneficial for each of you to go through the entire process yourself but have each other support, encourage, and advise each other as accountability partners.

Mentors can also play a crucial role in accountability. A mentor is someone with more experience who can guide you and hold you accountable. Finding the right Mentor involves looking for someone you respect and trust. They could be a teacher, a family friend, or even a local business owner willing to offer their insights. What's important is that your Mentor has achieved what you're looking to achieve and grown a successful small business from scratch so that they can give you insight and guidance from a place of specific experience.

KEY POINTS:

- Accountability is invaluable. When you verbally commit and speak your goal aloud to someone else, you show up and execute in a greater way to make sure you have something to show for yourself for the week.
- Your accountability partner's wins can help you get through an incredibly challenging week.
- Celebrating your wins with someone who's going through the same process feels even more powerful because they understand the significance of your wins.

ACTION STEPS:

- Choose your accountability partner (or Mentor).
- Start by scheduling a weekly accountability meeting with your partner (or Mentor). Pick a time each week and book it on your calendar. It can be an online meeting (Google Meet is free), or you can meet in person. These check-ins are brief but invaluable.
- Make a simple spreadsheet where you track your weekly accountability. Each week, you set the goal for this week, discuss your progress on last week's goal, share your wins for the week, and discuss the one challenge you have that you need support on to help you achieve your goal this week. Each person can take 5-10 minutes to go over their four accountability points.
- Make sure that each of you fills out your spreadsheet the night before your meeting so you get the most value from the time you're spending together. When you book the time in your Google calendar, link the accountability spreadsheet in the event and set a reminder for one day before so you can always fill in your accountability spreadsheet before your accountability meeting.
- Weekly Accountability Spreadsheet Template

SIMPLE EXAMPLE:

Weekly Accountability Spreadsheet					
Date	Your Name	Last Week's Goal	Wins To Celebrate	Challenge To Discuss	This Week's Goal

Wins and Rewards Matter

Whether it's the parade after the Superbowl, going out to dinner with the cast after a theater performance, or a bonus for a promotion at work - achievements are acknowledged with a reward everywhere you look. The reward is powerful, and the trick is to harness this power by starting to recognize and acknowledge your wins daily. When you see yourself winning, it creates positive momentum and shows you and your brain that you keep winning every day - and that momentum increases your forward motion on your business journey. For instance, Alex launched a coding tutoring service. When he reached his goal of teaching 50 students, he rewarded himself with a new laptop. This not only acknowledged his hard work but also reinvested in his business, allowing him to offer better tutorials.

When you recognize and celebrate your achievements, your brain releases dopamine, a feel-good hormone that boosts your mood and motivation. This creates a positive feedback loop where you're encouraged to continue working hard to experience that rewarding feeling again. Recognition also builds momentum. Each celebration acts as a stepping stone, propelling you forward and making the next goal seem more achievable. It's like climbing a ladder; each rung you reach gives you the confidence to aim for the next one.

The reward for your win doesn't have to be huge; it should be proportionate to your win. What matters is that you start recognizing, documenting, and acknowlededging the wins on a daily basis. One of my past mentors would always talk about the benefits of a brag book. That's what you're going to start today. Every day, write down at least one thing that was a win for you. Honestly, some days, you might have a ton to write down, and some days, not so much. You can talk about a win from today or a win from your past; it doesn't matter when you did it; what matters is that you write something down every single day. Maybe you aced a test or a project. Maybe you scored the winning point for a game. Maybe you shared your lunch with someone who didn't have any food that day.

When you start recognizing wins, you're training your brain to see them. What you focus on grows. When you look at the disappointments in your life - they multiply. When you look at the wins in your life - they multiply. It's like the old story of the red car. When someone talks to you about a red car, you suddenly start seeing them all around you. What you focus on grows. So, what do you want to focus on? When you start training your brain to see all of your accomplishments every single day, you're pre-programming yourself not only to identify them, but you will inevitably leverage that momentum and start creating more wins as you do this more often. It's literally inevitable.

Now for the rewards. Start a Google Spreadsheet for your rewards. Every week, make a time block in your calendar and start adding it to your rewards list. It can be a simple brain dump. It can be anything you enjoy - going to the movies, picking up food that you love, heading down to the beach or the lake for the afternoon, or going on a food adventure. You can also start listing larger rewards - like buying a pair of Jordans, an outfit, or an Apple watch that you've wanted. Start listing all of the rewards that bring you joy. Some people really enjoy items, and some people really enjoy experiences. There's no right or wrong here; it's about what you enjoy. Every week, when you're done brain-dumping and adding to your rewards list - go through and label them as small, medium, or large. You're going to be able to assign different rewards to your goals as you set them. When you achieve a goal, execute and celebrate. Don't skip this step—it is a huge hack for forward motion and increased momentum in your path to your business.

Incorporating celebrations into your routine is a key component for maintaining long-term motivation and continued success.

KEY POINTS:

- What you focus on grows.
- Recognizing and documenting your wins creates more wins.
- Celebrating your wins supercharges your ability to achieve the next win.

ACTION STEPS:

- Start a brag book today - on your computer, phone, or in a journal. Write down at least one win every single day.
- Create a list of rewards you would enjoy for small, medium, and large achievements, and book a Google calendar event every week to add to it. Link these rewards to your goals and make a plan to celebrate each win.
- Rewards List Template

At this point, you've already achieved a number of wins:

- Set your morning routine.
- Mapped out your time blocking on your Google calendar.
- Chosen an accountability partner and booked your weekly meeting.
- Set your first income target and make it a SMART goal.

- Started your brag book.
- Made a list of rewards and attach them to your goals.

Now it's time to earn your first dollars in your new business and set you up to hit that first SMART goal.

PHASE ONE: LAUNCH

EARN YOUR FIRST DOLLARS

To Read Or Not To Read

This Section is for you if you're a teen looking to start earning money in a new or existing business. But if you're already earning money in your business, I would still read this Phase because looking at something from a fresh, new perspective is invaluable. Sometimes, we get used to the way we've been doing things, and we miss opportunities that are sitting right in front of us. Maybe there's a new strategy in here that you've never tried, and that brings you new dollars. Read through this Phase and implement strategies that help generate revenue in your business.

We're here to walk through the steps to earn your first dollars in a new business. This isn't just about making a dollar; it's about picking a business you like that you're excited about and then confirming that you can actually make money in that business. All the pieces have to be there for you to succeed. Because after we set you up to earn your first dollars in Phase One, we talk about earning them more consistently and then how to make those dollars grow - that's covered in Phases Two and Three. But before we can get there, we need to start here. There is no business without revenue. So, let's jump into it.

THREE

How To Create Money From Nothing

Monetizing Existing Skills & Strengths

To find the right business for you, we start with what you already have - your skills and interests. Open up a spreadsheet, and let's start a list of your strengths, hobbies, and skills. Think about what you enjoy doing in your free time and what you're good at. What sports have you played? What subjects in school do you enjoy? Do you sing, dance, act, or play an instrument? Do you love planning and throwing parties? Are you artistic? Do you love photo and video - shooting and editing? Are you a great writer? Do you love kids? Do you love pets? Do you love food? Do you love to travel? Are you a great organizer or a great gardener? Do you love to clean or to build things? Are you great at calligraphy or illustrations? Do you love doing handy tasks around the house or maybe just running errands? Sit down for about 15 minutes and write down literally all of the things you know how to do - even if you get stuck for a minute or two, just keep writing them all down.

After you're done brainstorming on your own - review the list below to add additional skills that you have and the services you could monetize from those skills to grow your list further. There is some redundancy in the list, but it's because you might like one aspect of the skill and not another; maybe you don't want to groom pets, but you would want to sit pets or walk pets.

- **Tutoring**: Academic subjects like math, science, or language arts.
- **Pool Cleaning:** Skimming or vacuuming the pool or spa, balancing the chemicals
- **Mother's Helper:** Helping with kids or household responsibilities while the mom is home
- **Dog Walking**: Providing exercise and companionship for dogs.

- **Pet Sitting**: Caring for pets while owners are away.
- **House Cleaning**: Cleaning and organizing homes.
- **Lawn Mowing**: Maintaining and beautifying lawns.
- **Car Detailing**: Washing and cleaning vehicles inside and out.
- **Babysitting**: Childcare for families.
- **Cooking/Baking**: Preparing meals or baked goods.
- **Social Media Management**: Managing social media accounts and content.
- **Graphic Design**: Creating logos, flyers, and digital content.
- **Photography**: Taking and editing photos for events or portraits.
- **Event Planning**: Organizing and coordinating events like parties or weddings.
- **Guitar Lessons**: Teaching guitar playing.
- **Voice Lessons**: Offering vocal coaching and training.
- **Fitness Training**: Providing personal fitness sessions and plans.
- **Writing and Editing**: Social media posts and content.
- **Language Instruction**: Teaching foreign languages.
- **Tech Support**: Assisting with computer or tech-related issues.
- **Website Design**: Designing and developing websites.
- **Virtual Assistance**: Handling administrative tasks remotely.
- **Crafting**: Creating and selling handmade crafts.
- **Floral Arrangement**: Designing and arranging flowers.
- **Bookkeeping**: Managing small business finances.
- **Home Organization**: Decluttering and organizing spaces.
- **Video Editing**: Editing and creating videos for personal or business social media.
- **Pet Training**: Teaching pets new behaviors or commands.
- **Social Media Content Creation**: Creating engaging content for social media.
- **Interior Decorating**: Assisting with decorating and styling interior spaces.
- **Personal Shopping**: Helping clients shop for clothing or gifts.
- **Art Lessons**: Teaching drawing, painting, or other art forms.
- **Data Entry**: Entering and managing data for businesses.
- **Travel Planning**: Organizing travel itineraries and bookings.
- **Gardening Services**: Planting and maintaining garden spaces.
- **Handyman Services**: Performing minor repairs and maintenance tasks.
- **Virtual Tutoring**: Offering academic help online.
- **Elderly Assistance**: Helping elderly individuals with daily tasks.
- **Personal Fitness Coaching**: Offering workout plans and motivation.
- **Craft Workshops**: Teaching crafting skills in a group setting.
- **Social Media Ads Management**: Running ad campaigns on social media.
- **Proofreading**: Checking and correcting written content.
- **Poetry**: Writing poetry for proposals and wedding ceremonies.
- **Event Photography**: Capturing moments at events like weddings or parties.
- **Drone Photography:** Creating business videos through drone photography.
- **Meal Prep Services**: Preparing meals for busy individuals or families.
- **Voice Training**: Improving vocal techniques and skills.

- **Pet Grooming**: Offering grooming services for pets.
- **Podcast Production**: Creating and editing podcasts.
- **Digital Marketing**: Providing marketing services online.
- **Book Club Facilitation**: Leading book discussions and clubs.
- **Custom Illustrations**: Creating unique illustrations for gifts and events.
- **Computer Programming**: Writing code and developing software.
- **Virtual Reality Experiences**: Creating VR content or experiences.
- **Sewing and Alterations**: Repairing and altering clothing.
- **Event Coordination**: Managing logistics for events.
- **Mobile Car Washing**: Providing car washing services on-site.
- **Local Tours**: Offering guided tours of local attractions.
- **Homework Help**: Assisting students with homework assignments.
- **Decorative Painting**: Painting murals or decorative designs for homes or businesses.
- **Language Translation**: Translating documents or conversations.
- **Custom T-Shirts**: Designing and printing custom t-shirts.
- **Fitness Classes**: Teaching group fitness classes like yoga or Zumba.
- **Cooking Classes**: Teaching cooking techniques or recipes.
- **Mobile Tech Repairs**: Fixing smartphones or tablets.
- **Kids' Party Planning**: Organizing and planning parties for children.
- **Online Tutoring**: Teaching subjects through virtual platforms.
- **Custom Calligraphy**: Making personalized or custom calligraphy projects.
- **Event DJing**: Providing music and entertainment for events.
- **Dance Instruction**: Teaching dance classes or private lessons.
- **Art Commissions**: Creating custom artwork for clients.
- **Customer Service**: Providing customer support for businesses.

Because we're looking for the quickest way to earn your dollars - we want to work with what you've already got in terms of skills and talents. You can always learn new talents and grow your business further, or even develop into a new business - but first, we earn the dollars now.

ACTION STEPS:

- Pick the top 3 - 5 skills or services you are best at and would love to get paid to do every day.

You Make the Most Money When You Pick A Skill You Love

But it's not just about picking any skill that you have - you absolutely need to enjoy it. One of the businesses I set up for one of my sons was a website design business. It was so simple. We set up the business, the design templates, the sales script, the pricing, and every part of the business. It was so easy, and he kept saying he wanted to do it. But the truth is - he didn't enjoy it - so he never actually took action to start the business. He couldn't get himself to do it even though he knew it made sense and he could make great money.

We saw what was happening and made a change. He decided to start cleaning sneakers (high-end ones like Jordans) and then started flipping shoes. The difference was huge - not only did he jump into it, but you couldn't stop him from working on it. It was all he wanted to do and talk about. That's the difference. The skill set you pick for your business has to be something you enjoy and want to do because no matter what - if you don't really want to do it, if you're not really into it, you're not going to do it. And forcing yourself to do something you just don't want to do doesn't work out when we're talking about starting a business. The drive and the excitement have to come from you - no one can give it to you. That's the driving force behind everything in your business. Recognize that and choose something you're into because making money is easy as long as you like what you're doing. There is literally always a way to hit your financial goals, as long as you pick the right business that you enjoy.

So many various services that come from your skill sets are in demand all the time in your local community. Tutoring services for school subjects are always in demand. Many parents are willing to pay for extra help to ensure their children succeed academically. Graphic design services for small businesses are another great option. Small business owners often need help with designing logos, flyers, and social media graphics. Gig work opportunities, like assembling furniture or running errands, can also be profitable. Lastly, social media management for local entrepreneurs is a valuable service, as many business owners need help maintaining their online presence. It's about picking something you love, something you're really good at, something people need, and connecting the dots so that creates dollars for you.

Who Do You Want For Your Customers?

Now that you have an idea of what skill you enjoy and what you want to do for your business - we have to make sure we're able to get customers easily. There are a few different ways you can offer the same service to different customers. For instance, let's say you like photography. You can offer photography to individuals (consumers) for newborns, pregnant moms, families, couples, weddings, engagements, proms/ promposals, family reunions, birthday parties, and the list goes on and on. You can offer photography for businesses, such as professional headshots, product pictures, company staff pictures, corporate events, and client events.

The list goes on here as well. Let's say you enjoy drone photography. You could partner with a wedding photographer and offer drone services, or you could use your drone services for real estate photography, which a realtor needs every time they get a house they're looking to sell. All of these services can be offered from the one skill that you have and love. What's important is that you provide a service that you know how to do - let's say you take photos at a birthday party instead of newborn photography because you've never done that before. Focus on what you know and what you can do an excellent job at because the quality of the service you provide is everything.

First, let's take the skill you picked, and let's have chatGPT help us build out a list of services that you can offer from that skill so you can refine what it is you want to offer and that you have confidence you can provide with excellent quality.

Matching skills to business opportunities involves identifying what people need and how you can provide it. For example, if you're good at math, offer tutoring services to students struggling with the subject.

Here's a ChatGPT prompt to help you brainstorm:

"What are some ways I can monetize my skill in [insert skill] as a service business for my local community?"

Use this prompt to explore different ideas and find the best fit for you.

Now, in the ChatGPT prompt, there are easy ideas where you can earn money right away and more complicated ideas that would take a while to earn dollars. Pick the specific services that you enjoy and where you could get your first customer in a day or two. In that previous list - tutoring, homework help, or test prep would be easy to get customers right away, while building out a summer math camp might take you a bit longer. Focus on easy execution with high quality to get your first dollars; then, you can always grow from there.

Now, let's make sure that people are looking for your services to ensure you can easily make your first dollar and get your first customer this week.

KEY POINTS:

- It's easy to make money from nothing.
- The skills and talents you have are more than enough to create a business today.
- Make sure you pick something you love to do and are exceptional at doing.

ACTION STEPS:

- Make a brainstorm list of your skills and talents.
- Use ChatGPT to turn your skill set into a list of services you can offer.

The reason we focus on offering a service from your skills and talents is because you can earn the dollars very quickly in a service business. Service-based businesses often have lower startup costs and quicker revenue generation than product-based businesses. For example, starting a tutoring service requires minimal investment and can quickly bring in cash. Services like graphic design, social media management, and gig work are in high demand and can be easily started with little to no upfront costs.

Now - let's make sure people are looking for your services so you're set up to succeed.

Who Wants To Pay Me Today?

Imagine you're launching a pet-sitting service. You've got the skills and the passion, but how do you know if there's a demand? Start by identifying existing market demand in your local community. Check local social media groups on Facebook or community platforms like Nextdoor. Even if you don't use Facebook, your customers do- so you go to the social media platform where your customers live. Look for posts where people ask for pet sitters or discuss pet care services. This will give you a sense of whether there's a need for your service.

There's an easy way to do this without getting lost in the rabbit hole that is social media. Let's go with the pet services business and make sure we can get customers easily.

First, go to Facebook and create an account if you don't already have one. Add a picture of your face so people accept you in the local groups, and add your family as friends to show you're a real person.

Next, go look up your city name and join all the local Facebook groups that have your city name or the surrounding city names in them. You will be shocked and amazed at the amount of time that your local community spends and the number of prospective customers you find who are literally asking for the service you're going to provide.

Do the same thing for Next Door.

> Now, go to ChatGPT and use this prompt to get a list of services you can provide based on the skill you enjoy and excel at. We want the ChatGPT prompt to identify keywords that were searched for in your service business.
>
> "I am starting a new teen business, and I love caring for pets. Please list the top 15 services that people in my local community are looking for that I can offer in my new pet care business. "

Pick the services that you enjoy and that you excel at, and use those keywords and search terms to search for potential customers on local platforms. Use the search bar on Facebook and next door to find people who are already posting and looking for these services today and ready to hire you.

For example, if "affordable pet sitting" is a top keyword, search for it on the local groups on Facebook and Nextdoor to find posts from people seeking this service in your local area. We are going to show you exactly how to comment on these posts by offering your services and sharing your contact information. This strategy helps you connect directly with those in need of your service now. What matters is that you look for the services and you see that there are people ready to pay you right now for these services. When you look on Facebook groups and Next Door and find your potential customer - you're ready to move on to the next step. If not, adjust your services and skill set until you make sure you can find multiple recent posts of people looking for your services in your local community. This is how you set yourself up for success, making sure it's easy to get new customers now.

Now, if you look up all the local cities in your area and you don't find any Facebook groups or NextDoor groups, which is highly unlikely because they're incredibly active everywhere around the world... here is the way to adjust your business to still utilize all the strategies in this book. Choose a virtual service and select the closest geographical area to you, join all the local Facebook groups, and keep going with the strategy. For instance, instead of choosing a pet sitting or pool cleaning (both in-person services), choose tutoring (which can be done online), Virtual Assistant services, or Graphic Design and Social Media Management. There are a huge number of services that you can do with your skill set that you enjoy and operate virtually.

You can even use this ChatGPT prompt:

"I excel at [skill, talent or interest], what are 25 different ways I can offer a virtual service based on my skill set to start my own teen business with no money out of pocket?] or [What are the top 100 most in-demand services I can offer virtually to start my own teen business with no money out of pocket?"

Play with the responses and the prompts until you find something you enjoy and excel at. Then, make sure there is high demand (a lot of people specifically looking for your services) in the local Facebook groups that you join before moving forward to the next step to start your business. Making sure to get this part right is the difference between easily hitting your revenue goals or having a much more difficult road ahead of you.

KEY POINTS:

- There are people in your local community right now who are ready to pay you for this service.
- Only offer services where you can provide the highest quality to make sure that customers come back and use you again.

ACTION STEPS:

- Search on Facebook and NextDoor to find customers who are ready to pay you for your services now.
- Make sure there are multiple inquiries online in your local groups so you can have the easiest time getting your first customer.
- Adjust the services you offer to make sure you can do a great job, you love providing those services, and customers are looking for your services now.

Knowing How Much To Charge

Next - we need to know how much to charge for your services. The best way to determine this is to pretend that you're the one looking for your services. Let's say you know how to play piano, and you're exceptional at it. You have a piano at home you would love to give lessons. Great - now you need to pretend that you're a parent looking for a piano teacher. Go online and find 3 - 5 people in your area that you would consider as a parent to teach your (imaginary) kids how to play piano. How much do they charge? How often are the lessons? How long are the lessons? Do you go to their house/business, or do they come to yours? Do they charge differently if the lesson is here or there? Gather all the information and understand how much a parent would have to pay for that service.

Now, since you're great at playing piano, identify what's best for you. How often should a kid take lessons? What is a competitive rate for you to charge based on the other people providing the service in your area? Will you only go to their house, or are you okay with some lessons being done at your house since some parents won't have a piano in their home? What kind of discount or promo can you offer for a new student? 50% off your first lesson? But two lessons and get the 3rd one free? Which makes sense to you? You want to offer a promo in a way where it would be a no-brainer for the person to take you up on that new student offer, but you still make money. Do not offer your services for free. I know people might recommend you do that, but don't do that. People value what they pay for more than they value what they get for free. More importantly, the skills and talents you possess are highly valuable. Know your value. Charge for your value.

Here's a quick and important point for you to remember. A product business, like selling sodas and candy, has product cost. If you're selling a service, you still might have some product costs (like mulch if you're doing lawn care services), but the main cost is the time for an expert (you) to provide the service. When you're setting up your service business, you don't have to buy any products - but the time it takes to provide the service is an actual cost. Let's say you get a ton of customers, and you can't provide the service yourself to all of them - which is a great challenge that you will have as long as you keep implementing the steps in this book. You will need to be able to pay someone else to do the service at an hourly rate and still make a profit as the business owner. We have to make sure that when you're setting your pricing from the very beginning, you take staff cost into consideration, or else you might be setting up your whole business to lose money. Ensuring profitability is about understanding your profit margins.

Let's start setting your pricing, and then we'll walk through how to make sure it's profitable.

> You can also use a ChatGPT template to determine your rates:
>
> "What is the average rate for [services] in [your city]? How often should I provide services per week? What introductory discounts can I offer to attract new clients?"

Use this information to set competitive rates that are appealing but also ensure profitability.

Choose your pricing and a couple of ideas for promos to attract new customers so you can really set yourself up for success as much as possible. Now - let's walk through the easiest possible way to map out the process so you have a clear plan of what to do when someone wants to pay for your services. In the next section, we're going to talk about how to accept money from customers who want your services, but right now, we need to walk through how you're going to set up the service itself.

Let's stick with the piano lessons. Rates are going to vary by location, experience, etc, so this is just an example. Let's say, for beginner lessons, that you're going to offer:

- Two lessons a week for 30 minutes each, and each lesson is $40.
- So the retail price for your first two week's lessons is $160 for four lessons in total—two 30-minute lessons per week for two weeks.
- But let's say your intro offer is 50% off your 2-week intro package.
- Now - they pay just $80 for four lessons, which should be a no-brainer.

Piano Lesson Duration	Lessons Per Week	Price Per Lesson	Number Of Weeks	Retail Price For 2 Weeks
30 minutes	2	$40	2	$160
New Customer Promotion				50.00%
30 minutes	2	$20	2	$80

Note: Each of the examples used in this book will be linked to a template you can use to calculate your numbers. When you click on the template link, you will see the example and then a place to enter in your numbers to calculate them for your business. Each of the spreadsheets are setup with formulas, so only enter your numbers into the gold fields and everything will calculate for you automatically. When you click on the Template link, it will pop up to make a copy so you can play with the spreadsheet and put in your own numbers and it will save into your Google Drive.

Now - quick profitability check - If your retail rate (not your new customer promo rate) is $40 per 30-minute lesson, then you're essentially making $80 an hour. Let's say you hire someone you know who is a skilled piano player like you and pay them $30 an hour to give the lesson. You might ask why they would take $30 when you would get $80. It's because they don't have a business; they don't know how to get customers, market, or manage the whole piano lesson business. There's a huge difference between how much a business charges customers vs. how much an employee gets at an hourly rate to provide the service. But back to our example. $80 hourly is what the customer is paying you (Revenue), and $30 is your staff rate (Expenses), so your profit is $50 an hour. Yes - this is a profitable model. It's okay to offer an intro rate that's less to attract new customers based on your ability to provide such a good service that they want to stay with you for the long run.

Piano Lesson Duration	Retail Lesson Rate	Retail Hourly Rate	Staff Hourly Rate	Gross Profit Per Hour
30 minutes	$40	$80	$30	$50
New Customer Promotion				**50.00%**
30 minutes	$20	$40	$30	$10

The whole purpose of an intro offer is to attract new customers so you can start your business, and through your exceptional quality of service (piano lessons), your responsiveness, your wonderful communication, and your care that your customers have experienced in the first two weeks - now they want to stay with you forever. And - they want to refer all of their friends to you for lessons as well. So, for this to succeed, you have to provide exceptional service (piano lessons) and take great care of your customers through communication, etc.

Now you have an easy framework where you can identify what to charge for your service, the basic framework for your service (2-week intro package), and a new customer promo, and you're ready to move forward to actually reach out to local customers and get your first dollars in this business. Adjust as necessary for it to make sense for your service. You already have this skill and know what's best in terms of the length and frequency of this service. Use ChatGPT to help, but set the service up to benefit the customer and set you up for success so they want to continue to use you and your service.

KEY POINTS:

- Pretend you're a customer looking for your service online right now so you can understand how much to charge and how often to provide the services.
- Make sure you factor staff expense into your pricing to make sure your rates are profitable.
- An intro discount or promo attracts new customers, but the way to make sure you're successful is to offer such an excellent service that they keep coming back and bring all their friends.

ACTION STEPS:

- Determine your pricing and the way you offer your service.
- Create your new customer pricing and package.
- Service Pricing Promotion Template - Launch

Providing A Great Service So The Customer Pays You Again And Refers Others

Now - let's make sure you have a really basic structure for what to do when you get there so your customers are highly impressed with your professionalism and your service, and they can't stop talking about how great you are to every person they know. Let's take a different example and say you're going to set up a lawn care service.

Apply these same structures to map out the simplest possible process to deliver your service for your new business.

> Here's a ChatGPT prompt to break down the simplest way to provide the service to a new customer:
>
> "What are the simplest steps to deliver a high-quality [service] to a new customer in [your city] for my new teen business?"

Key points to remember here are this - only offer services where you have the supplies and equipment, or factor the price of buying supplies from the dollars you earn from getting your first customer. An example of supplies you would buy to serve your first customer would be flowers they want you to plant or mulch they want you to use. Do not spend a bunch of money to set up your business before you ever make any dollars. Ask to borrow lawn equipment from your parents or offer different services until you earn enough money for the business to pay for the equipment you need. Maybe you have a lawn mower but not an edge trimmer, earn enough money mowing lawns and make sure you like and want to keep running the business, then use the money you earned in the business to buy the edge trimmer so you can offer that service and make even more money.

KEY POINTS:

- Don't spend any money to make money. Work with what you've got to get your first customer and earn your first dollars; then, you can choose to spend those earned dollars to buy equipment and earn more money with that equipment.
- When a customer is ready to hire you for your services, you have to know the best way that you can deliver your service so your customer has a great experience, wants to hire you again, and wants to refer you to all their friends.

ACTION STEPS:

- Map out the simplest way to provide your service with the skills and equipment you have now once someone wants to give you money.

When starting out, focus on doing as little as possible to earn money quickly. You have to know how much to charge and how to provide the service, and now we have to set up some business basics so you can look professional and people trust that you will do a great job if they decide to work with you.

Minimum Effort, Maximum Impact

You will find that people in your local community will want to hire you to support a teen setting up a new business - which is incredible. But you have the opportunity to accept their kindness, impress them with your professionalism and quality of service, and earn their business for life. Setting up just a few basics will again impress your first customers and show them that you have a real business that will be here to serve their needs today and for the long run. Let's walk through the biggest impact steps you can set up and how it should be done within an hour or two.

1. Online presence:
   - Many new service businesses today only have an Instagram, and it's an accepted way to show your credibility and showcase some of your services. You can set it up in a matter of minutes. When you're choosing your handle, try to use the main keywords for your service and your city or area. For instance, [city][service]. We live in South Orange County, so an example would be LagunaLawnCare for your lawn care business or SanJuanSwimming for your business offering swim lessons. Coming up with something functional will help you more than coming up with a fancy name. This whole process is supposed to be the quickest way to revenue, so only spend a few minutes coming up with your IG handle.
   - One thing we're going to do right now is buy the domain for your business name. We're only going to take a few minutes to do this and set it aside for later. We don't need to get fancy and make a website, but we do want to make sure you're set up for success later. So, whatever you pick as your IG handle, make sure the domain name is available, and go to Name.com or Godaddy.com to buy that domain name. You don't need to do anything but purchase the domain, and it should cost you less than $20 to buy it.
   - Now, back to the IG you set up; add a couple of pictures of the service you provide, either that you've taken yourself while doing the service or from a free picture site like pexels.com. You can set up a Google calendar block for 30 minutes a week to add content and post, but remember - that doesn't directly generate revenue for you, so that's not something you need to spend a lot of time doing right now. As you provide service, you can take before and after pictures or pictures of the service you offer and post them during this weekly time block.
2. Business email:
   - Set up a free Gmail account for your new business that matches the name you chose for your IG handle. When you make a Gmail for your business, all of the spreadsheets and docs you create should be attached to this Gmail account to keep things organized. You've probably already been using Google Workspace for years in school and know how much you can do with the free tools. Now, you get to take all the time you've spent for school on Google Workspace and apply that knowledge to your business to earn dollars. Here's a template to start listing all the different online accounts and passwords you're setting up in this Chapter so you can stay organized and always have your business information available to you quickly.
3. Business Phone:

- Set up a free business phone number with Google Voice; it should be linked to the same Google Business email you set up. You can use the web version and download the app to your phone. Keeping customer questions, inquiries, etc., separate from your personal number helps you make sure to get back to them as soon as possible and keep things organized. Anytime you market your services or respond to inquiries, always use your business number.

4. Separate Checking Account:
   - Separating your business dollars and your personal dollars is extremely important. We will get into this more later, but you will absolutely set yourself up for success by opening a new checking account for your business now. Set up a business savings account as well so you can transfer extra profits every month to put them aside in a dedicated account. If you're a minor, you will likely need a parent to be on the account as well, but make sure you set up the checking account and get a check card attached to that account to use for business expenses when you need to use the money you earned to buy things for your business. Choose any bank you prefer, but make sure they don't charge any fees at all and don't require a minimum balance. Bluevine and Novo are both great options and currently don't charge any fees.

5. Taking Payment:
   - The two simplest ways to take payments for your business are Venmo and PayPal. We will talk later in this book about accepting credit cards, which is highly beneficial for your business, but again - we want the simplest and quickest way to get to your first dollars. Make sure you connect PayPal and Venmo to your new business checking account. Again, you might need a parent to assist you, depending on your age. For consistency, make sure the Venmo handle matches the business name you used for your IG handle and the email address you created.

6. Simple Service Summaries:
   - You can offer exceptional service, but if the customer thinks you're coming for an hour and you think you're only coming for 30 minutes because of a simple miscommunication, you're not set up for success. Setting clear expectations before you accept payment is key. You can literally ask ChatGPT to make a basic summary for you and send it to them by text and email for confirmation so that you're on the same page.

Here's a ChatGPT prompt template like this:

"I'm starting a new teen business for [service]. Please create a simple summary of the proposed services that I can send to my new customer." Simply have them reply to confirm that they've read the summary and have the same expectations, so you are set up for success."

KEY POINTS:

- Basic business tools set you up for success by both looking professional and proactively communicating so you set the right expectations for your service.
- It should only take you a couple of hours to set up these business basics, and our focus is to do only the minimum amount of setup to have the maximum impact.

ACTION STEPS:

- Set up all the business basics above so you can move forward and get your first customer now.

Business Owners are Action Takers

Imagine you have a great idea for a dog-walking service. You've done your research, and you're ready to get started, but something's holding you back. You want everything to be perfect before you launch. Here's the thing: waiting for perfection can paralyze you. The benefit of imperfect action is that it gets you moving. Action, even if it's not perfect, allows you to see what works and what doesn't - that is valuable data. You learn more from things that didn't work than from things that did. Each misstep is a lesson that helps you adjust your strategy. So, don't wait until everything is perfect - there is no such thing. Get out there and start offering your service. If something doesn't go as planned, adjust and keep moving forward.

Quick decision-making is an essential skill for running a business. Analysis paralysis can be a real problem. You spend so much time thinking about what to do that you end up doing nothing. Successful business owners make decisions quickly but don't just leap without looking. They gather the best information they can, review it swiftly, and make informed choices. Once they act, they collect data quickly to see what's working and what's not. Then, they pivot as needed. The overarching theme here is speed. The faster you can make decisions and act on them, the quicker you'll see results. For example, if you notice that your dog-walking service isn't attracting enough clients on Next Door, try different Facebook groups. If dog walking doesn't have much traction, try dog grooming or dog sitting, etc. The key is to keep moving forward, taking action, and adapting.

KEY POINTS:

- Taking imperfect action allows you to learn and improve.
- Quick decision-making is critical to the success of your business.

ACTION STEPS:

- Identify the most important action you need to take right now to move forward and earn dollars and take it.

You have already taken so much action and made so much progress on your business. Every single action you've taken should be in your brag book, and your rewards should be rolling. Every step you've taken so far is so we can take this next step. It's time to get your first customer and earn your first dollars. Let's do this.

FOUR

Earning Your First Dollar This Week

R emember stepping onto the field for a big game, or onto the stage for a big performance, or even sitting down to take a test that you know you're ready for. That moment is filled with confidence, a little bit of fear, and a sense of relief and accomplishment when you're on the other side. Starting your business and earning your first dollar feels a lot like that. It's thrilling, a bit nerve-wracking, but incredibly rewarding once you get it right. So, let's talk about how we earn money without spending any money.

Don't Spend Money To Try And Make Money

When you're just starting, the idea of spending money to make money can seem inevitable. That's where pre-selling comes in. Pre-selling is the process of selling a product or service that doesn't yet exist to ensure your revenue and validate your business idea. It's getting people to commit to buying your service before you've fully developed it. This approach has several benefits, especially for cash flow.

We have already touched on this with the lawn care service, but let's take another example. Imagine you're starting a video editing service to help clients post social media content to attract new customers to their business. Instead of signing up for video editing software upfront and then hoping to find clients, you start by making sure you get a new customer. We break down the steps below, but basically, you find the people already posting and looking for this service; you respond to them with your offer, explain why you're the best person to help them, offer them a discounted rate for being a new customer, and secure payment. This way, you earn money before you spend any money. You're essentially getting paid to start your business, which is a huge advantage (Source 1). Now - this only works when you're offering a service that you are exceptional at providing and utilizing a skill that you're already well versed in so you can provide a quality service to your client. You can only pre-sell a service when you know you can deliver and meet the client's needs.

Another example is Zoe, who wanted to start a custom T-shirt business. Instead of printing a bunch of shirts and hoping they'd sell, she reached out to people online who were looking for custom printing and offered them a discounted rate. This validated that there was interest in her custom shirt printing business and provided her with the funds to print the shirts. By pre-selling, Zoe avoided the risk of having unsold inventory and ensured she had cash flow from day one.

One of the key reasons you should never spend money in a new business until you've secured customers and received payment is to avoid unnecessary spending before you're 100% sure that you want to do this specific service as a business. When you start reaching out to customers and offering the service that you chose, you're excited, you're super motivated, you get your first customer and earn your first dollars, and you can't wait to actually provide the service and then get a bunch more customers. Pre-selling ensures that the business you chose is aligned and that you want to proceed with offering this service. Most importantly, it helps you manage your cash flow better. Most people don't have unlimited cash to invest in a business before earning a dollar. Developing the skill to make money from nothing and knowing that you can do that in multiple different ways at any time in your life is an invaluable skill.

KEY POINTS:

- You can make money from nothing.
- Pre-selling is the best way to ensure positive cash flow and minimize risk.
- Securing your customers before you spend any money also ensures you want to do this business and that you're excited to launch and grow it moving forward.

ACTION STEPS:

- Do. Not. Spend. Any. Money. Before. You. Earn. Money. In. Your. Business.

Creating Your Easy Sales Pitch

We're here to make the process of earning your first dollar as simple as possible so you can do it as quickly as possible. That's why we're going to get your first customer by responding to posts online so you can reach out to as many people as possible in as little time as possible and get your first customer. As long as you find people in your community looking for your services before you choose your business, you will inevitably get a customer just by responding to posts. The business is there; it's just a numbers game until they pick you. So, let's walk through it.

When you're trying to get a new customer, you need to explain what you do, who you do it for, and why you're the best choice for them to pick. Let's say you're offering a tutoring service, and you see someone post that they need an algebra tutor for their kid who's struggling in class. Your pitch should explain why you're the best choice and why you meet their need. Here's an example. "Hi, I'm Alex. I'm a senior at [local high school], and I've been in honors math classes all through high school [this shows your experience]. I started a local tutoring business to help younger kids who are struggling so they can raise their grades and not feel like they keep falling behind [this meets their specific needs]. I have an intro rate for new families to make sure we're a good fit, and we can help your son get what he needs to bring his grades up. Feel free to text or call me at [business phone number] so we can make sure to talk about what you're looking for and the best way to support your son in getting his grades up. I'd love to chat with you more. Do you have time to chat today?" You want to ask a specific question and tag the original poster in your response to hopefully begin a conversation.

One of the most powerful parts of responding to people who have already posted online and are looking for your service is that they explain their needs more fully. This is how you'd change the post in a different situation where they're looking for help with honors classes tutoring. "Hi, I'm Alex. I'm a senior at [local high school], and I've been in honors math classes all through high school [this shows your experience]. I started a local tutoring business to help kids manage the workload and pace of honors classes so they continue to be set up for success [this meets their specific needs]. I have an intro rate for new families to make sure we're a good fit, and we can make sure to set your son up for this class and his AP path overall. Feel free to text or call me at [business phone number] so we can make sure to talk about how your son is currently doing in his honors class and what the path looks like going forward for him. I'd love to chat with you more. Do you have time to connect today?"

To tailor this to your specific business, you can use this simple ChatGPT template to help you craft your pitch:

"I'm a [age]-year-old running a new teen business offering [service]. I've seen a recent online post where someone is looking for [service] for [who is the service for]. I want to respond to this post to offer my services. Can you help me draft a response that includes why they should choose me, an intro offer for new customers, and the best next step for them to take and why?"

Personalize it to fit your service and make it sound natural.

The key points to remember are to keep it brief, focus on the value you provide, and tailor it to the specific information you're able to see from their posts and the comments they've replied to on that post. Your pitch should be simple and authentic and point the prospective customer to the next step to make sure they reach out to you or to get permission for you to reach out to them, either by phone or message. The more posts you respond to, the more conversations you have, the better you will be at this skill. This skill, sales, is one of the most valuable skills you can develop in your life.

You want to post as many responses as possible online for people searching for your service and list your business phone number. Other people who are looking for the same service will utilize the search function in the group find that post find your number, and reach out to you directly. How nice will it be to get incoming texts on your business phone number for people who are specifically asking you for your service? The more you post online to these responses, the more you'll get incoming inquiries about your service on your business phone number.

KEY POINTS:

- Tailoring your sales pitch shows the prospective customer that you understand their needs.
- Being authentic and caring in your pitch shows that you value the business of this prospective customer, and they will get high-quality service from you.
- Your response should concisely show your experience, how you meet the specific needs they're looking for better than anyone else, have an offer that's a no-brainer, and the specific action they should take next.
- You want to post as many responses as possible online for people searching for your service and list your business phone number.

ACTION STEPS:

- Search online and start creating a basic response template for you to use to respond to people looking for your services online so you can get your first customer as quickly as possible.

The Fortune Is In The Follow Up

Prospecting, following up, and closing the sale can be simple if you have a clear strategy. We have just walked through the simplest possible strategy to help you get your first customer. Understand, though, that sales is a numbers game. How many people do you need to respond to for you to get your first customer? That is called your first sales conversion metric. Open up a spreadsheet so you can start tracking how many people you respond to and who they are so you can follow up. People get busy, and their priority might not be getting someone to provide this service. Your service might be 1 out of 100 things they need to get done. People appreciate and need your follow-up to help them get through their very long task list. When you're starting out and want to get your first customer, the more posts you respond to, where people are looking for your services, the better.

Make a spreadsheet and write down the name of the group where you found the post and the name of the person who is asking for the service. Then, you'll be able to track how many people you reached out to every day and how many people it takes for you to get a new customer. Let's say you respond to 16 people and get two customers. That's fantastic. That means, on average, for every eight people, you get a new customer. If your average customer pays you $100 a month for lawn care and you want to make $500 a month. Then you just need to get five customers. If you reach out to 8 people and you get a new customer, on average, then you just need to reach out to 40 people looking for lawn care, and you would, on average, hit that $500 monthly number. Do you see how this is the best kind of math? Now - your averages become more accurate the longer you're doing this.

	Leads	Customers	Sales Conversion %
	16	2	12.50%

Service	Monthly Rate	Revenue Goal	Customers Needed	Leads Needed
Lawn Care	$100	$500	5	40

Averages are always more accurate with more data. Now, let's say that you reach out to 16 people and get two new customers. But let's say you also follow up with the 14 people who haven't signed up with you yet, and you get one more customer from simply following up. That changes your numbers completely. Now, all of a sudden, instead of 2 customers in 16 responses, you have three customers in 16 responses. That makes your monthly revenue goal even easier to hit.

	Leads	Customers	Sales Conversion %
	16	3	18.75%

Service	Monthly Rate	Revenue Goal	Customers Needed	Leads Needed
Lawn Care	$100	$500	5	27

Every day, you put the date on your spreadsheet and track who you reached out to so you can track your numbers and have a clear and easy way to follow up. Most people don't follow up; that's why they say that the fortune is in the follow-up. When you follow up with someone who is looking for your service, they know you're reliable, consistent, have great communication, and are organized. They have a much higher probability of selecting you for the service. Keep following up, respectfully and consistently, until you get a polite no.

The fortune is in the follow-up - so it's a very lucrative skill for you to develop. If you've reached out and haven't heard back, send a friendly reminder.

Here's another ChatGPT prompt for follow-up:

"Hi [Name], just wanted to check in and see if you've found someone you love for [service] or if you're still looking for the right person. I'd love to connect with you if you have time today. Feel free to text or call me at [business phone number]. I have time to chat today, and I would like to get this set up for you and take it off your plate. Let me know if you have any questions, and I look forward to speaking with you".

Rephrase the follow-up into your own words and personalize it with any information that's available in the post and the post comment replies.

KEY POINTS:

- The fortune is in the follow-up stage for two reasons. One - most people don't consistently follow up. Two - it really increases your value in the eyes of your prospective customer when you follow up.
- Sales conversion metrics are some of the best math that exists. It's math to make money and so much fun to calculate and leverage to hit your revenue goals.
- Track your reach out and your sales, and you will identify exactly how to reach your revenue goals.
- The more you reach out, the more accurate your averages will be, and the more they'll improve, as this is a skill that you get better at with practice.

ACTION STEPS:

- Make a tracking spreadsheet to track all of your reach out and sales on a daily basis so you can get your sales conversion metrics.
- Leads Tracking Template
- Reach out to as many people as possible every day so you can get your first customer and earn your first dollars as quickly as possible.
- Close your first sale and deliver a great service before you move on to the next Chapter.
- Leads and Sales Tracking Template - Launch

WIN:

YOU HAVE OFFICIALLY
STARTED A NEW BUSINESS
AND EARNED YOUR FIRST DOLLARS.

You have accomplished more by utilizing the first
Phase of this book than the vast majority of adults.

Post your win, celebrate, and enjoy your reward.

You should be incredibly proud of yourself.

Make a Difference with Your Review

UNLOCK the Power of Leading By Example

"Success is not just what you achieve, but what you inspire others to achieve."

When you take action and share your success with others, you make it easier for them to follow in your footsteps.

Be the person who makes a difference for the next teen entrepreneur.

Now that you've started your journey and seen what's possible with *Earn Money In Your Teen Business*, it's time to help someone just like you—someone curious about starting a teen business but unsure where to begin.

My mission with this book is to make the process of building a successful, cash-flowing teen business simple and achievable for everyone. But I need your help to reach more teens who need guidance.

Most people pick their next book based on reviews.

So, I'm asking for your help—leave a review and share your wins.

At this point, you have a huge list of the wins you've accomplished, from your morning routine to your accountability, to identifying which skill you're monetizing, to earning your first dollar, and the list goes on and on and on.

You could help inspire the next teen to follow their dreams and take that big step toward becoming a business owner.

Your review could help:

- One more parent provide the support their teen has been asking for to start their business.
- One more teen believe they can actually do this because they saw what you were able to accomplish, and that was the difference maker for them.
- One more young entrepreneur start the income stream they need to buy their first house.
- One more teen figure out what they're best at so they can monetize their skills now and know they have what it takes to start a cash-flowing business.
- One more teen start earning now to create their 7-figure reality.

To make a difference, simply scan the QR code below and leave a review:

I also want to celebrate your wins. I read every single one of the reviews that get posted, and when you share your wins, post pictures or videos about your wins and your takeaways from this book, I get to see and celebrate with you.

Some wins make you feel like you want to cheer and scream at the top of your lungs because you're so incredibly proud of your accomplishment.

I totally get it - I still feel that way about my wins too. Post so we can all celebrate them together.

You're an action taker and have accomplished so much - even though you're just getting started... I can't wait to read all about it, and stay updated every step along the way.

Chris Rosenberg

P.S. If you haven't gone to Amazon and posted a quick review yet, go there first and then keep going for the bonus....

If you've already posted a review from earlier in the book - go and update it with your wins so people can keep cheering you on!

P.P.S. BONUS: If you'd like to cheat sheet of all the spreadsheet templates and resources listed here, you're welcome to send us an email at wins@meridianpub lishinghouse.com.

Make sure to include your wins so we can celebrate you as well!

PHASE TWO STABILIZE:

EARN CONSISTENT DOLLARS

After Your First Dollar Comes Many, Many More

You've done it. You've earned your first dollar in your new business. That's a huge milestone, and it's something that a lot of people never achieve. Think about it—how many people can say they've taken an idea, put in the work, and turned it into actual money? It's a big deal. But here's the thing: earning that first dollar is just the beginning. To build a stable, successful business, you need to ensure that revenue keeps coming in consistently. This is where the fun begins.

You picked your business, you got your first customer, and you earned your first dollars. All of those things are incredible. Or maybe you've been running your business for a while, and you skipped the Launch Phase and came straight here to Stabilize. If you come across a concept you're unfamiliar with or a key metric in your business that you haven't identified, like your sales conversion ratio, go back and work through the steps in the Launch Phase. This book builds on specific steps. Create the most solid foundation for your business by making sure you have every step solid in your business.

Stabilization is all about making sure the dollars come in consistently. It's amazing to have a business you enjoy and a service you love and be able to make money from nothing. That's a skill and talent that few people in the world understand how to leverage. But now - the game is to learn how to create those dollars on a monthly, weekly, or even daily basis if you choose. There are core elements to your business that cause it to create consistent dollars, and you can look at them like the legs of a table. If your legs aren't solid - your table won't stand on its own. The legs to stabilize any business are leads, sales, and service. Without leads, you have no potential customers. Without sales, you have no revenue. Without great service and an ability to provide a quality customer experience - they'll never repurchase, and no one else will either. But the solid tabletop that brings everything together - is profitability. Many businesses can have leads, sales and service, and still not make any money and go out of business. The numbers have to set you up for success. So, to create stabilization in your business and have the strongest table - you need to have leads, sales, service, and profitability. That's how you're unstoppable.

Cash flow is like the lifeblood of your business. Without it, everything grinds to a halt. You might have the best service in the world, but if you don't have a steady stream of income, it's incredibly hard to keep things going. That's why it's key to focus on creating consistent cash flow. When revenue is stable, you have options - you can make plans to grow, you can hire, and you can count on your business month in and month out. The good news is that there are so many ways for you to grow your cash flow and create that stabilization, and we're going to walk through the steps now.

The Roadmap To Hit Your Consistent Dollars

One of the best things about business is that everything is laid out for you like a roadmap. A lot of people get confused and frustrated and spin in circles, but it's because they went off the map. Anytime you want to achieve anything in your business - go back to the roadmap. The roadmap lays out exactly what you need to accomplish and how you're going to do it. So - let's talk about earning more consistent dollars. What does that mean to you? How much do you want to earn consistently?

In the last Phase - Launch, you earned your first dollars. Let's say your goal to earn consistent dollars is $1,000 a month, which is about $250 a week. I'm picking that goal as an example for easy numbers - your goals might be more or less. There's no right or wrong goal, and there's no use comparing your goal to someone else - you're the only person that matters in this discussion - what is your goal? That's what's important. Let's take the example of $1,000 a month to create stabilization in the business. This Phase Two Section of this book is going to help us design our roadmap so we can stay on track and crush this Phase of the book.

In Phase One, you calculated your sales conversion ratio. As a quick reminder - you were tracking - how many people you reached out to (leads) and how many new customers you got as a result of those conversations (sales). For instance, let's say you reached out to 4 new people a day and responded to their post online where they were looking for your exact service. In the span of a 5-day week - you reached out to 20 people. As a result, you have two new customers. That would mean that you had 20 leads and two sales. Two sales divided by 20 leads means that you have a 10% sales conversion ratio. That means, on average, for every ten people you have a conversation with about your services, on average one of them will be a customer. We also talked about how this number goes up as you grow your business because you get better and better, but let's use this example for now.

Sales Conversion Ratio			
Leads Per Day	Leads Per Week	Sales Conversion %	New Customers Per Week
4	20	10%	2

In Phase One, we also talked about how much you make from one customer to make sure you're profitable.

Let's say that your business is offering tennis lessons, and you charge $50 an hour, and lessons are twice a week. For your business, one customer is worth $400 per month. $50 an hour for two lessons per week equals $100. An average month is four weeks, so $400 would be the monthly rate for one customer. That means that to exceed your $1000 per month goal, you need three customers (at an average of $400 each), which would give you $1,200 in revenue each month.

Sales Conversion Ratio							
		Leads Per Day	Leads Per Week	Sales Conversion %	New Customers Per Week		
		4	20	10%	2		
Tennis Lesson Duration	Lessons Per Week	Price Per Lesson	Number Of Weeks	Retail Monthly Rate	Revenue Goal	Customers Needed	Revenue Achieved
30 minutes	2	$50	4	$400	$1,000	3	$1,200

Now - if we go back to our sales conversion metrics, we know that you need ten conversations to get one client.

So - to achieve $1,200 in revenue, you need three customers (sales), and to get three customers (sales), you need to have 30 good prospective customers (leads).

So, if you keep doing exactly what you were doing in Phase One - reaching out to 4 people a day and responding to their inquiries for service online, you would get 30 leads and three new customers in literally less than eight days.

Sales Conversion Ratio						
	Leads Per Day	Leads Per Week	Sales Conversion %	New Customers Per Week		
	4	20	10%	2		

Tennis Lesson Duration	Lessons Per Week	Price Per Lesson	Number Of Weeks	Retail Monthly Rate	Revenue Goal	Customers Needed	Revenue Achieved
30 minutes	2	$50	4	$400	$1,000	3	$1,200

Service	Monthly Rate	Revenue Goal	Customers Needed	Leads Needed	Days Needed To Reach Goal		
Tennis Lessons	$400	$1,200	3	30	7.5		

That is what we call a roadmap to revenue. And it's fantastic.

Now, suppose you keep up that same level of activity. In that case, you can literally grow your business by that same $1,200 per month in new revenue by consistently adding 30 leads a month and three sales a month... but we'll leave that discussion for Phase Three of this book, the Scaling Section.

Now you know how many leads you need and how many sales you need to get to your consistent dollars and reach stabilization in your business.

Most adults have never created such a roadmap, nor do they have an understanding of this concept of stabilizing the legs of your table for the benefit of your business.

Now that you have the framework of the roadmap, pick your goal and easily calculate what your roadmap looks like for your business. Use the same Google Doc you used before and update it with this new goal. Print this new goal up on a sheet of paper and post it in your room by your goals from Phase One. Then - let's work through this Section of the book to crush your goal. Remember - read, execute, read, execute, and so on. Let's go secure that first leg in your table.

Note: You and I both already know that you're going to crush this $1,000 monthly revenue goal, and your business is going to continue to grow. Once you start earning around $2,000 a month, ask your parents for a referral and schedule a call or an in-person appointment with a tax advisor. Once you're earning about $2,000 a month in your business, you're going to have to file a tax return, which is nothing to worry about. The tax advisor will walk you through every step of the process, and because you've already set yourself up with separate business accounts and been keeping track of every step, you're already set up for success. Later in this Section, we're going to talk more about business expenses, especially as you grow. Every step of it is broken down, so you have everything you need for your tax advisor. Just know that once you hit about $2,000 a month in revenue, you should proactively schedule a consultation to be set up for success for you and your business.

KEY POINTS:

- Once you get your first customer, you have what you need to design the roadmap to hit whatever Revenue goal you desire, and you know exactly how to get there and how long it will take.
- You've already taken this exact set of action steps to get your first customer; now it's just about repeating the process to hit your Revenue goal.
- The more leads you create, the more sales you convert, the better you get at those steps, and the easier it is to accomplish your Revenue goal.

ACTION STEPS:

- Set your monthly Revenue Goal and use your Sales Conversion metrics from Phase One to create the roadmap to achieve your Revenue Goal.
- Go crush your goal.
- Revenue Goal Template

FIVE

More Interested Customers

O ur singular focus in this Chapter is to hit the number of leads you need to hit your revenue goal. For this example, it's all about getting to 30 leads. Now, you might be tempted to spend a bunch of time posting on social media, creating content, and building a brand, and that's not to say that those things don't have benefits. But let's talk about the different kinds of marketing.

Getting The Biggest Bang For Your Buck

Whether you've been in business for ten days or ten years, you have a specific amount of resources to use. Those resources are usually time and money, and when you're starting your business, you tend to have more time than money. But both of those resources are highly valuable. Whether you're investing your time or your money, you need to invest it in a way where you get the highest return on your investment (ROI). If you spend 3 hours a day holding a sign on a busy street corner hoping people will be interested in your tutoring business and, after a 5-day week (15 hours of your time), you have 1 interested person (lead). That's not a great ROI. Compare that with the strategy we taught you in Phase One, the Launch phase of this book, where you responded to people specifically looking for your service. Let's say you spent the same 3 hours a day, but instead of 1 lead holding a sign on a corner, you got 15 leads in that same 15 hours spent in a week. That's a much better ROI and a much better return on your investment of time. Your time is incredibly valuable - invest it in your business in a way where you're set to get the greatest return.

ROI marketing is different from brand marketing. While ROI marketing aims for immediate revenue generation and measurable results, brand marketing focuses on long-term brand awareness and reputation. Imagine you're responding to someone on Facebook looking for family photography services. That's direct revenue generation because you're engaging with a potential customer who's ready to buy. On the other hand, posting on Instagram and hoping someone who needs a family photography service will see it is more indirect. Both have their place, but for small businesses with limited resources looking to maximize their revenue as quickly as possible, ROI marketing gets you there quicker. It's like choosing guaranteed dollars over the possibility of dollars.

The core objective of ROI marketing is to maximize the return you get from the money (or time) you spend on marketing efforts. Think of it as a way to make every dollar you spend on marketing bring you back more money. Whether you're spending time or money on marketing, you always want to set yourself up for the highest ROI. Because your time is valuable, your time is money.

Finding More People Who Want To Pay You Today

Different businesses serve different groups of people, and it's key to understand who your customers are so you can find them to offer your services effectively. For instance, if you're offering babysitting services, you're likely going to have moms as your customers, and they're going to be on Facebook and NextDoor; they're going to want someone reliable, honest, and trustworthy, so they feel like their kids are safe when they're being babysat. Instead, let's say you offer private baseball lessons; your customers might be dads who want to make sure you have the specific knowledge and experience to teach their kids the developmental skills they need at this point in their baseball life, that you get along with their kid, and that their kids will not only listen to your advice but be open to incorporating your coaching into their baseball game. Understanding your target market is like having a treasure map. It shows you where you can find your ideal customers and allows you to communicate with them better so they want to hire you for the services you're offering instead of your competition.

Understanding why prospective customers need your service can be the difference between them reaching out to you or your competitor. Your target market needs your service for very specific reasons. They have pain points that your service can alleviate. For instance, if you're offering a babysitting service, your target market might be young parents who haven't been able to go out on a date night forever, feel guilty leaving their kids, and don't want them to be parked in front of a TV all night. Those are some of their pain points, and they're concerned that if they pick the wrong babysitter, they won't know if they made the wrong decision until it's too late. You can post and address these points specifically in your marketing, and it can be the difference maker in having them move forward and choose you. You can talk about how, while they're having a date night, their kids will be having their own playdate - playing board games, cards, or basketball in the backyard, whatever is age-appropriate. You can say that your kids are going to have so much fun they're going to be begging you to go on another date night next week. This not only alleviates your target market's pain points, but it also makes it where they want to reach out to you, they feel a sense of comfort and trust, and you set yourself apart from other babysitters out there and have a much better chance to get them as customers.

To get a clearer picture of your target market, use this ChatGPT template:

"Can you help me identify my target market for a [specific service] in [your location]? Include age, gender, interests, and common challenges they face."

This will help you tailor your marketing efforts to reach the right people.

Analyzing the competition can also work in your favor. Remember how we had you search for your service online, just like you were one of your own prospective customers? Look at your current competitors and the people in your community who provide complementary services. For example, if you're offering pet sitting, check out local dog walking or grooming services. See how they market themselves and what their customers like about them. You can use this information to help serve your customers even better. Maybe you can offer drop-in checks for their dogs while they're out of town because they want them to stay home instead of being boarded at a facility. You can find out so much information about your local competitors and community, and you can use that key information to help make the social media posts you will post everywhere this week.

Use this ChatGPT template:

"I'm starting a new teen business offering [services] to [target market] in [area]. Please provide me with my target market, my local competitors, their top qualities, and their biggest downfalls so I can set myself apart from the competition."

This will provide so much more information that you can then have ChatGPT help you understand where you stand and how to position your business for success. By knowing your competitors' strengths and weaknesses, you can tailor your services to meet the needs of your target market better.

KEY POINTS:

- Knowing who your customers are, where to find them, and what their specific needs are, increases your probability of converting them into customers for your business. Said another way, the better you know your prospective customers, the higher the chance they'll actually become your customers.
- Knowing your prospective customers' pain points and addressing them in your conversation (whether online or in person) builds trust and confidence and increases the probability that they will choose you to provide the service.

ACTION STEPS:

- Search the posts online looking for your service and start to identify your prospective customer's pain points and how you can best address them.
- What can you easily provide to your customers to be a better offer than your competitor?

Reaching Out To Those Customers Looking For You Now

In Phase One, we covered where to find local customers actively looking for your services and posting online, ready to hire the right person. You made sure to choose a business with multiple inquiries for your service and demand in your local community for your service. Now, let's talk about the best way to prioritize your time and create easy steps to hit that number of 30 leads to hit your revenue goal this month.

Set up a time block in Google calendar for 30 minutes a day, every single day. If you can, post online and respond to inquiries to ensure you hit your target lead count to hit your goal. Next - create a spreadsheet to track the local Facebook groups in your area. Make sure to create columns in that spreadsheet to list the group name, the group link, how many people are in that group, when you're allowed to post in that group, and what date you last posted in that group. Creating that spreadsheet will help you keep things easy and organized, making hitting your 30 leads a month easier. When you go to Facebook and click on the groups section, start searching for your city name, click to join every group with your city name, and add them to your spreadsheet to track. Each of these groups has people in your community looking for your service and posting to find the best person for them to hire for your service. Every community group on Facebook has different rules. Some groups allow you to post and advertise your services anytime, some will only allow it on a certain day, and some won't allow it at all unless someone is specifically looking for your service. Join all of the groups and list them on your spreadsheet, making sure to list if you can post and what day you're allowed to post on your spreadsheet to make things really easy.

Two key ways to easily leverage Facebook groups to hit your revenue goal this month exist. Remember when I mentioned to you in Phase One the most recent business we built in our family, the family meal delivery business? We used the exact same strategy for our business to get new customers. We started our business in September, and in November, we earned over $10,000 in revenue that month. The business is there in your local community; you just need to know how to reach the people who are looking for you, get in front of them (leads), have them choose you (sales), and provide a quality service (service). Let's go through the two key ways to leverage Facebook in less than 30 minutes a day.

Every single day, you're going to search Facebook for the keywords that best fit your services. Let's say your business is lawn care. Come up with a list of the top keywords your customer is searching to find your service: lawn care, mow lawn, landscaping, gardeners, etc. When you search on Facebook, adjust the filter so it only shows your groups and pages, or else you're going to be seeing posts from areas outside your local community.

> Here's an easy ChatGPT prompt for your keyword list. List the keywords in your Facebook spreadsheet to stay organized and get the highest ROI on your marketing time in your business.

> "What are the top 10 keyword phrases that people in [local area] are using on Facebook to get a referral for a [service] for [target market]. For example: "What are the

top 10 keyword phrases that people in [city] are using on Facebook to get a referral for a tutor for their kids."""

KEY POINTS:

- Identifying and using the right keywords for your service in local Facebook groups improves your chances of finding customers ready to hire you.

ACTION STEPS:

- Set aside 30 minutes daily specifically to engage with your local community on Facebook. This includes searching for posts asking for your service and responding to them directly. Use your Google calendar to stay focused and productive during this time.
- Use your spreadsheet to determine when you can post in each group. Set reminders in your calendar for the days you're allowed to post in each group.
- Draft a few engaging posts that showcase your services, special offers, or customer testimonials. Use visuals whenever possible, like before-and-after photos or video snippets.
- Facebook Posting Calendar

Let The Customers Come To You

The second strategy is to post online on the allowable days in those local Facebook groups. Now - I know this might seem more like the brand marketing we were talking about, but let me break down the benefits for you. When you're posting in the same groups that people are asking for your specific service, many of those people will use the search in that group and find your post offering your service. When you post online in the group, you get comments and get to talk about your services with prospective customers. There is a specific way to get the most benefit from these posts and simplify the process. Every week, you're going to set up your post, and every day, you're just going to copy and paste it.

1. Decide what you'll offer as a promo for new customers (10% off, buy 2 lessons, get 1 free, etc). We covered in Phase One and how to make sure your new customer promo keeps you profitable.
2. Have a basic graphic or picture so people notice you and stop scrolling. You can make a basic graphic in Canva for free that is professional and reflects your business service and your target market. Use one of Canva's free templates and adjust it for your business.
3. Always ask new customers to take an action. Post the Google Business phone number you set up in Phase One and tell them to text you for the promo code. You do this to ensure you get your prospective customers' contact information so you can follow up and convert them into customers.

ChatGPT prompt:

"I just started a new teen business for [service]. Please create 4 different posts I can use for social media to get new clients and offer a [discount] for new customers. Please make the post short but effective with a call to action to have them text me for a promo code. Please make sure to address their typical pain points and what the benefits of using me would be and encourage them to give me an opportunity to support a new local teen business in their community."

Every day in your time block, search for people looking for your service in your local area using your keywords. Then, you're going to copy and paste the same post that you prepared for the week in the groups that allow you to post for that specific day using your template and graphic. Then, as comments and responses come in, reply to them promptly so you can hit your 30 leads this month.

Notice that we focused a lot on local Facebook groups because your potential customers are already there and are actively looking for your services. If you choose a business and you realize that there is not a high demand in your area for that business, and you are not set up for success and able to hit your goal of 30 new leads in a month through simple posting and reaching out to people who are already looking for your service - pivot and choose a different service business that you also love. Here's a quick example. If you love underwater basket weaving (ridiculous, I know, but go with me on this), does it matter that you provide the best service? Does it matter that you have the best, most competitive rate? Does it matter if you're looking and posting every day for hours? No. None of that matters. It's like offering a service to shovel snow out of driveways while you live in Southern California. No one needs that service. No one is looking for that service. Set yourself up for success. Your business has to meet a need already in high demand in your local area.

There are a ton of people in your local community looking for services every single day and ready to pay someone who does a great job, and even more than that, they want to support a teen in their own community with a new business. But you have to make sure to pick a business and offer a service that is in high demand in your local area, or you are not setting yourself up for success. Don't be attached to the specific service you're offering, and refuse to pivot. Be attached to doing something you love (each of us loves doing many things, and we are each talented at many things we can offer as a service), and be attached to the success of your business.

Whether you're offering a personal service - private lessons, house services, errands, etc. or a business service like content creation, social media management, graphic or logo design, website development, tech support, etc. You can still find your local prospective customers on Facebook groups and NextDoor. These small businesses are owned by individuals in your local community and are all very active on Facebook and NextDoor.

From week to week, you can mix up what you post but keep the same content for the whole week, so you only spend time making that post once a week and also make sure those 3 tips above are always part of your post: Promo code, graphic and call to action.

Here are 5 examples of different styles of posts you can create:

1. Limited time offer (for a Holiday or event)
2. Customer Testimonial (written or as the graphic in your post)
3. Pro tips for your service that your customers would benefit from
4. Before and after results
5. Contest or giveaway (this can be your call to action instead of a discount code)

Remember, your target is to get 30 new leads a month, and by getting 4 leads a day, as your numbers have shown, you can accomplish the entire goal in about 7 days. But you set that goal for the full month. So keep your pace of 4 leads a day and see where that lands you for your 30-day goal. Remember - the more data you track, the more accurate your numbers. Let's see your numbers after 30 days of leads, sales, and service in your business. Generating 30 leads in a month, converting that to 3 new customers in a month, and crushing your $1,000 revenue goal is completely achievable. But remember that might come with 3 leads on one day, none the next, and 1 day after that. What matters is that you take consistent action, track your efforts, and watch the numbers. As you look at your numbers after 1 week, 1 month, 3 months, 6 months, etc., you'll see how much better you're getting at generating leads and closing sales. You'll see which kinds of posts work better than others and what the biggest differences make for your customers to respond to your comments and then choose you. Every business is different, every service is different, and every community is different, but that's a good thing. You are growing your business and becoming great at running your specific business in your specific community - you get better each and every day, and you actually get paid to get better.

KEY POINTS:

- Posting regularly in local Facebook groups increases visibility and engagement, helping you convert more leads into customers.
- Using a call-to-action with a promo code and great graphics to stop the scroll helps attract attention and gives people the financial incentive to contact you.
- Offering a service that is in high demand in your local area will ensure that your business is set up for success.

ACTION STEPS:

- Book time each day on your calendar to post in local Facebook groups that allow service promotions, focusing on groups where people are actively looking for your services.
- Create four posts at a time, one for each week, with a promo code and graphic, and reuse them every day throughout the week. Track responses and adjust based on what works.
- Step back and look at the demand in your area. If, for any reason, you chose a service that does not have high demand in your area, pivot to a more in-demand service while still focusing on something you enjoy.

Follow Up Marketing

Building a prospective customer list is worth its weight in gold for a business. When you reach out to local customers and provide them with a promo code for a discount on your services, you get their phone number, and you're able to follow up with them. Even if only 1 out of 10 leads signs up as a customer from the initial inquiry, you have an opportunity to keep in touch with that lead and likely have them do business with you in the future. The person who texted you for the promo code is interested in your service and chose to give you their phone number. You can call to follow up with them to see if you can convert them to a customer, and we'll cover sales in more detail in the next Chapter - but here's an easy tip I want you to incorporate into your marketing follow-up.

There are holidays of some kind every single month. I want you to tie in a promotional offer with a monthly holiday for your business and text out a promotional code to everyone you have in your Google Voice messages. As your business grows, you will outgrow Google Voice based on your number of leads and your ability to text them. We'll cover this in the next Section about scaling. For now, while you're still growing and building at 30 leads a month, Google Voice is an excellent and free option. Let's say you offer lawn care services, and the 4th of July is coming up soon. You can offer a holiday promo - maybe 10 or 15 % lawn care to celebrate the 4th of July and text out that promo to your leads. You can go to ChatGPT to help you create the promo and give you ideas, and then you can edit and finalize it yourself. This holiday / promotional offer can also be the basis for your weekly social media post.

ChatGPT prompt:

"I have a teen [service] business and I want to text out a discount offer for [discount offer] services for the [Holiday] if they book this week. Please create a short text with a clear call to action to convert my lead into a customer."

Remember, the fortune is in the follow-up. I've had people on my lead list for months, and they are so impressed by the persistent, respectful, consistent follow-up they receive from our business that they become customers. Remember - they can always ask to be removed from your list by simply replying unsubscribe or stop. Don't worry; when people ask to be removed, it means they weren't going to purchase your service anyway. You want the greatest ROI on your time and money, and you want to spend it following up with people who truly want and need your service. The rest of the people on your lead list, there's a reason why they haven't asked to be removed, and they're choosing to stay on your list and get your monthly promotions... its because they're interested in your service, but they haven't made the time to get to you on their very long to-do list yet. We ask for phone numbers to text promo codes because it's simple and easy, and there is a much higher response rate on text via email. As you grow your business, you can grow an email list and incorporate that as well, but remember, we want to focus our efforts on the highest ROI, and that's what we're doing step by step.

KEY POINTS:

- Creating a prospective customer list is crucial to following up and converting leads into customers, even if they don't sign up immediately.
- Consistent follow-up through text, especially tied to holiday promotions, helps re-engage leads and encourages them to become paying customers.
- Monthly promotions tied to holidays create an opportunity to offer discounts and maintain communication with your leads, increasing the chances of conversion.

ACTION STEPS:

- Set up promo codes to encourage leads to share their phone numbers. This will allow you to follow up later and potentially convert them into paying customers.
- Send monthly promotions tied to specific holidays to your lead list, offering discounts. Use a clear call to action to encourage bookings.
- Calendar time to regularly follow up with leads who haven't yet converted, offering new promotions or reminders while allowing uninterested leads to opt out.

The Power of Getting Knocked Down & Getting Back Up

People are usually applauded and celebrated for the greatness they've achieved. But what about the struggles along the way? Were there applause during the struggles? Or doubt from the onlookers? Silent, or maybe not so silent, comments about whether or not that person will ever achieve their goal? Every single person who has achieved greatness was thought of as crazy before they achieved their goal. There's a reason for that. When you have a vision in your mind of what you're going to achieve - no one can see that vision except you. And until you achieve that vision, all anybody can see is that you haven't achieved it yet. Every step you take, every action, every possible setback is a step on the path to your greatness. You are the only person who needs to see and know the greatness that you are meant to achieve. And you need to know that you are in the company of greatness. Every person famous for their achievements has been exactly where you are right now, and they're cheering you on.

No matter what area of life you consider, there are incredible people that faced setbacks. Steve Jobs. Oprah Winfrey. Michael Jordan. Anthony Bourdain. J.K. Rowling. Think about Steve Jobs. Before Apple became a household name, Jobs faced numerous obstacles. He was even fired from his own company. Yet, he used these failures as stepping stones, returning to Apple to lead it to unprecedented success. Another iconic figure, Oprah Winfrey, was once told she was unfit for television. Instead of giving up, she pushed forward, eventually becoming one of the most influential media personalities in the world. These stories illustrate the concept of "failing forward," where each failure is seen as a step toward success. Normalizing failure is crucial because it's a natural part of any entrepreneurial path. It's not a sign of defeat but rather a learning opportunity. Average people are afraid to fail.

Exceptionally successful people accept it as part of the process on their way to achieving their inevitable success and use it to propel them forward faster.

Young entrepreneurs often face typical fears that can hold them back; even though they're the same fears many adults have, teens have an advantage - they can usually break through those fears even better than adults. What matters is that you build the skill set to move forward in action even through the fear. Some people think the fear goes away and that's how people can move forward in action. That's a false assumption. The fear doesn't typically go away; it's just that the desire to achieve the goal is so much greater that it dwarfs the size of the fear - and that's how successful people can move forward, even with fear - their desire and commitment and sheer determination outweigh the fear - and they get to their goal that way. There is no achievement without failing.

Successful people fail more times than other people even try to accomplish anything. There is a famous poem by Theodore Roosevelt called The Man In The Arena that talks about how those on the outside will criticize the strong man in the arena when he stumbles, but that there is no achievement without stumbling and how those who are on the outside never know victory or defeat, because they haven't even tried... they remain on the outside. Criticism usually comes from those who have not achieved or tried minimally and allowed the failure to stop them. Those are not the people in your life to discuss or consult about your business. Those are great, kind people, but they don't understand. You wouldn't go talk to your Spanish teacher for help with your Science final - they don't know how to help you.

Talking about your business is exactly the same - you talk about your business to people who have accomplished similar things in their businesses. Every single one of those people has experienced their own version of disappointments and setbacks, and they've persisted and succeeded - because they haven't given up. Learning from each failure is the secret key to success. Every setback provides a specific lesson on what didn't work and how to adjust your approach. When we don't learn the lesson, we get the same setback again and again until we learn the lesson and implement the learning. When you find yourself frustrated, step back and think to yourself, "What is the lesson here? What am I supposed to be learning to grow past this?" Reflect on your setbacks, identify the lessons, and consider how to incorporate the new learning to propel you forward. Each lesson brings you closer to success. Embracing setbacks as part of the process builds a skillset and propels you forward in your progress.

The only way to truly fail in this entrepreneurial path is to give up. The key to this success is to move forward and take action, and the numbers work in your favor to create your desired income. As long as you execute the steps on this path, you are literally set up to succeed. Even if one person or another doesn't choose to become a customer, there's a person right behind them who's been looking for you and your business and can't wait to become your customer.

One of the most important things we discussed at the beginning of this book was The Mental Game and the things we instituted into your routine to set you up for success in your Mental Game. There are proven things to get you back onto the right track with your mental game. We'll cover a few here, but you need to develop and refine your own list because everyone is different. Creating a toolbox of different hacks to increase your vibes and get back on track is a key element to success that many adults have yet to figure out.

1. Your brag book and your sheet with your income goal on it are posted by your bed. Pull out your brag book now and look through the pages. Even if you only wrote one small sentence as a win every day since you began, you have tons of things listed in there. You achieved every single one of those things, and you're literally just getting started. Imagine how much you will have accomplished in another month or in another year, and imagine what your income will be like by then. Training your brain to see and celebrate your wins is more important in being a business owner than almost any other path in life. When you're a business owner - you are the heart and soul of your business, and it's your Mental Game that keeps you going. Go take a few minutes and write down some things in your Brag book cause there are definitely wins you haven't added yet. On days when your mental game isn't where you want it to be - grab your brag book and start reading through all that you've already accomplished. I bet a couple other things will start coming to mind for you to add to that list. We all have those off moments.

2. Soundtrack of My Life - there are specific songs you listen to, and no matter what mood you're in, they shift your energy and get you smiling, singing, dancing, moving, or whatever - they get you on your game again. I had a coach years ago who told me to start my own soundtrack and only put songs on there that got me going when I listened to them. I started to make that soundtrack (on Spotify, for free) that same day, and now whenever I think of a song or hear a song that does that for me - I add it to my soundtrack. I also go on Spotify sometimes and use autosuggest and add to it. When I look at my soundtrack while writing this, it's over 35 hours long. Sometimes, I add a song, then it plays, and it doesn't really do it for me, then I remove it. That's okay. When I feel off and go to play my soundtrack, it shifts my vibe, and I almost immediately feel better, and I can get back on track.

3. Laughter is one of the most powerful tricks to shift your vibe. When you feel off, it's a bad feeling, and when you laugh, really laugh, it fills your whole body, and if you're doing it right, it's a full belly laugh and moves through your whole body. So whether you have a favorite movie or show, clicking it on to shift your energy can really shift you out of that space and start moving you into a better vibe.

4. Taking a walk and moving your body also allows you to shift out of a bad vibe. Usually, when we're upset or disappointed, our whole body feels contracted. Our shoulders are tight and up by our ears; we might be crossing our arms or closed off across our whole bodies. Getting up and walking out the door and around the block to smell the fresh air, feel the sun on your face, and change the scenery has a huge impact. For some people, it's going for a run, doing a workout, or jumping in the water for a swim; at its core, it's simply moving your body. It helps clear your mind

and change your vibe, and you can feel your whole body start to release from the frustration you previously felt.

Start noticing what changes your vibe - the things that change it for the good and the things that change it the other way, too. The more you notice, the more you're in control of how you feel and what vibe you're on. Earlier in the book, when we talked about morning routines, we talked about how important it is for you to feel good and set yourself up for the day. Even in the middle or the end of the day, when you get off track, your ability to do any one of these things to reset your vibe makes all the difference. When you're in a great mood, you're able to do more and accomplish more - when you're not, nothing tends to go right. Be mindful of where you're at and what vibe you're on, and as you develop your ability to notice and set your own vibe, you'll see your business grow exponentially in the same direction.

KEY POINTS:

- There is no success without failure; understanding how to fail quickly and fail forward will set you up for much greater success.
- Each setback teaches you a critical lesson about how to better achieve your goal. Incorporate the lesson and keep moving forward.
- One of the most important muscles to build to achieve success is learning how to play the Mental Game. Identifying a list of ways to help you level up in your mindset (brag book, soundtrack, etc) and shift back into a good vibe is a skill that will catapult your success throughout life.

ACTION STEPS:

- Make a list of the elements that level up your Mental Game. Brag book, soundtrack, moving your body, etc. Start to notice when your vibe is off and use these tools to get back onto your good vibe. Keep using and growing this list on a daily basis.

SIX

The Most Valuable Skill You'll Ever Learn

S ales isn't just about making money; sales influences every aspect of your life, from personal relationships to professional opportunities. However, developing sales skills will directly impact your income growth more than any other skill.

Everything in Life is Sales

Understanding the importance of sales can open up a world of possibilities. Think about it: every time you persuade someone, you're selling. Whether convincing your parents to extend your curfew, negotiating a better grade with a teacher, pitching a project idea in class, or asking someone out on a date, you're using sales skills. Effective sales involve active listening, which means really hearing what the other person is saying and not saying it and responding thoughtfully. It's about excellent communication—being clear, concise, and engaging. And it's about creating a compelling, persuasive argument showing why your solution best fits their needs. Sales skills allow you to identify what is not said (an underlying objection) and address it to win the person over. In the curfew example, let's say your parents say you have to be home at a certain time. They don't say that they're worried about your safety, but you know that your safety is their unspoken concern (underlying objection).

When you're negotiating to stay out an extra hour on Saturday, you address that unspoken concern by saying where you're going to be, who you're going to be with, and exactly what you're going to be doing to assure them of your safety - if you have underlying trust in your relationship with your parents, and you address their underlying concern, they're much more likely to say yes. This is exactly how sales works and how you win over new customers. Underlying trust with active Listening, excellent communication, and addressing their underlying concerns that are unspoken, when done correctly, gets you the sale. Think of how this applies to safety when you're offering babysitting, or reliability when you're doing lawn care, or the ability to coach a student effectively in academic or sports lessons - addressing the underlying concern of the prospective customer and getting them to trust in you and your service is how they say yes to your service.

Every day, you have countless opportunities to sharpen your sales skills. When someone is talking to you, focus on what they're saying and try, and when they're done talking, repeat a couple of key items from what they said and ask a really good follow-up question. Active Listening is a rare skill, and people will be impressed and appreciative that you're actually listening to them. Active Listening builds trust dramatically and makes the other person want to do the same for you, which is a huge benefit in a sales situation. You can practice with your teachers, parents, and friends - your conversation will be different when you're with friends versus with your parents, but the skill is the same. There are key communication and sales skills that can set you up for massive success in life - real active Listening is a great one. When you're selling your services to prospective customers, they will have all kinds of personalities, so practicing your sales skills with a wide variety of people will help you be able to sell your services to all kinds of people. Understand what they want and what's important to them, and incorporate what they want to achieve into your proposed solution. For example, if you're discussing a group project, listen to your teammates' ideas and then present your own in a way that aligns with their goals. This makes them more likely to support your suggestions.

Improving your sales abilities can also come from simple, everyday interactions. When ordering food at a restaurant, practice being clear and polite, and use the server's name when responding to them. When asking for help, explain why you need it in a way that makes the other person feel valued. These small actions build your confidence and hone your skills. You'll find that the more you practice, the more natural it becomes to sell your ideas and persuade others. You will be shocked at how powerful these skills are and how they impact every aspect of your life.

One golden rule in sales is to underpromise and overdeliver. Some people mistakenly promise the whole world to get the sale, but they've already lost by setting unrealistic expectations. Let's say you're trying to get a new student for your tutoring business, and because you want the customer so badly, you start saying anything to get the business; by the end, you've promised that this kid, who's currently failing the subject will end up with an A in the AP class in their failing subject due to your magical tutoring. You just kept talking more and more to try and get the business, but really, you lost before you ever started, and it's because you set expectations so high; even if you did an incredible job, it still could never meet your expectations.

You're always better off telling the truth, being honest, and setting realistic expectations. Let's take that same failing student. You honestly talk to the parent and say, we're gonna work together to figure out the problem and get them back on track. It's not about just passing this class; we have to address the real issue of why s/he is failing and make sure they'll be okay with fixing their grade this semester and that it doesn't happen again next semester. Lets get them understanding the material and getting into a rhythm so they can keep up with the homework and be setup to do well on the tests. You didn't promise any kind of grade. You said you'd get to the root of the problem with the help of the parents and want to set the kid up for success. It's honest, it's achievable, and people respect them.

Some people think too little of others; they think they can say anything, and it doesn't matter. But the truth is, people respect honesty and understand if you're the right person for them when you speak to them honestly and intelligently about your service. Let's say in that same example, with the kid failing, you brought them up to a C, a passing grade in that semester, and they were able to keep the same pace and ended the next semester with a B-. That's a huge win for the kid, the parents, and you. Did you get them to be a straight-A student? No - but you clearly gave the kid and the family the help that they needed, and it showed in the results. You've exceeded their expectations, making them more likely to refer you to others in a similar situation.

Underpromising and overdelivering builds trust and creates raving fans for your business. So many people OVER-promise and UNDER-deliver that if you just do what you say you will do, you will outperform 99% of your competition. If you go beyond that and under-promise and over-deliver, your customers will be so impressed they'll never stop talking about how impressive you and your business are. This principle applies in results, like tutoring or timelines, like doing a family photo shoot, promising the proofs in 7 days, and getting them back in 3 - every business can underpromise and overdeliver and win the expectations game with customers.

KEY POINTS:

- Sales is literally integrated into every aspect of your life.
- Active Listening is a game-changer in all relationships.
- Underpromising and Overdelivering can be the difference between creating a raving fan out of your new customer and an unhappy customer, all because of incorrect expectations.

ACTION STEPS:

- Practice Active Listening in your daily conversations and notice the difference. This is an invaluable muscle to build in both your personal and business relationships.

Closing the Sale: Techniques and Best Practices

At this point, your primary way to attract prospective customers is online through conversation and possibly through text or phone follow-up. You've gotten them to reach out and say they want your service. You've used active Listening and persuasive conversation when discussing your services, but they haven't yet become a customer. This last point is called closing the sale, and there are a number of ways that people do this to convert a prospective customer into a paid customer.

Any kind of sale covers the same basic initial steps every time. Based on how we structure your online marketing and focusing on responding to people who were already looking for your specific services, a lot of this was done online, but it's important to review the key steps so you keep those same key elements in every interaction, whether it's online, text, phone call, or in person.

- The first step is to engage with people genuinely; this is often called building rapport. Smile, ask how their day is going, and listen to their responses. This creates a connection and makes them more comfortable.
- Next, identify the decision-maker. If you're talking to a group, figure out who is most interested in buying. Maybe it's the person asking the most questions or showing the most interest.
- Understanding customer needs comes next. Ask questions to uncover what they're looking for in your service. If they're looking for handyman services, do they want someone available for a few hours? Do they want someone to do a bunch of small jobs or be able to lift heavy items? Tailor your pitch to show how your handyman services meet their specific needs.

Effective closing techniques can make all the difference. There are a number of different sales closes. One powerful method is the assumptive close. Continue the conversation under the assumption that the customer has already decided to buy. As a side note, both of our boys have been using the assumptive close on us as parents since they were very young. For instance, you might say, "Would you like me to disassemble the desk and move the cabinets on Saturday, or just do the desk?" This assumes they're buying and pushes them toward a decision. The same principle applies to the lawn care business, "Would you like to mow the front and the backyard on Saturday, or just start with the front yard for now?" When you ask it like that, the person is giving you an answer on how much work they're going to give you, not whether or not they're going to use your services at all.

Another technique is the urgency close. Create a sense of urgency with limited availability. You might say, "I only take on a certain amount of students to make sure I can give them the support they need during the semester. I'm setting up my last spot this week - let me know if you want me to put [your kid] down for that spot." This encourages quick decisions because most people don't want to miss an opportunity. The summary close is another great option. Recap the benefits and then ask for the sale. For example, "So, you mentioned that you want me to come by and clean the pool weekly so you always have it ready to use during the summer and never have to worry when people stop by at the last minute. We'll make sure to come by every week on Wed afternoons at 5:30 cause that works best for you and your family, and we have that new customer promotion for 10% off for you today. Would you like us to start this Wed [list the date]?"

When you utilize any of these closing strategies, it's important to move into the sales confirmation right away. You start confirming the customer information; you make sure you have their name, address, phone number, and email correct, and they say yes to confirm each one of these pieces of information. We always take payment upfront, then you go ahead and say, I'm sending you a Venmo request for $X right now; let me know when you get it so we can ensure we're all set up and confirmed. Then, send the Google calendar event to the customer's email with the summary of services in the calendar Event notes.

People expect to pay for your services, and they're used to the payment part of the sale. Later in the next Chapter, we're going to walk you through how to set up credit card payments, which are incredibly beneficial to your business, but for now, make sure that you're getting payment upfront, just like we covered pre-selling and the summary of service in Phase One. Expectations for your service and payment need to be taken care of from the start, and then all that remains is for you to provide exceptional service to your new customer so they want to continue with your business and refer you to all of their friends.

As discussed earlier in this Chapter, handling objections, whether spoken or unspoken, is an inevitable part of some sales conversations. Listen actively to any concerns they may have. If someone says, "I'm not sure about the price," acknowledge their concern and ask a question. You can assume you know what they think, but you know what happens when you assume. Ask them, "How so?" Always ask for more information until you understand the actual concern so you can address it properly. You might think their concern is that you're charging too much, but they might really be concerned because you're charging too little, and they're assuming you don't have enough experience to provide a good service. When you fully understand their concern, you can address it properly because you chose a business where you're really good at providing this service - you're an expert at this service, and the customer is not an expert. So listen to them, and answer them honestly and with confident expertise. Either you get the customer, or you learn from the conversation. Either way, you and your business benefit.

We covered earlier about how the fortune is in the follow-up. Continuing to follow up with potential customers who didn't commit immediately is where you clean up compared to your competition. Look through your texts in your Google Voice and see if there's an opportunity to follow up on a past conversation. Maybe someone wanted to book you for Saturday morning, and you just got a spot open, so you send a follow-up to let them know. Maybe a prospect wanted you to offer edge trimming, and you just bought an edge trimmer, so you can follow up and let them know that service is available now and that you thought of them. Being honest, authentic, and sincere in your follow-up is something people appreciate and really remember. It makes all the difference. The ironic part is that being a great salesperson is honestly all the same basic qualities as being a really great person. Being thoughtful, establishing an honest interest in someone, actively listening to what's important to them, offering insightful suggestions and help, and consistently reaching out and connecting with them - these are all the great qualities of being a great friend and a great person.

KEY POINTS:

- Engaging genuinely and asking thoughtful questions helps you build trust and understand what the customer is looking for, making it easier to tailor your pitch.
- Proven Sales Techniques, such as the assumptive close, urgency close, and summary close, help guide prospective customers toward a decision.
- Actively listen to customer concerns, ask for clarification, and address objections honestly and professionally.

ACTION STEPS:

- Practice using the assumptive or urgency close in conversations to encourage quicker decisions from prospective customers.
- After closing, confirm customer details and payment and send them a follow-up confirmation via calendar or text to ensure clarity and professionalism.
- Book a 30-minute window each week on your calendar to review past conversations with potential customers who didn't commit right away and follow up with new offers because the fortune is in the follow-up.

SEVEN

Revenue Generation Is Everything

R evenue is the money your business earns from selling services. It's essential for a business's survival because it covers costs, pays employees, and allows for reinvestment into the business. Think of revenue as the fuel that keeps your business engine running. Just like a car needs gas to move, your business needs revenue to operate and grow. Without it, you can't pay for essentials like supplies, marketing, and, most importantly, pay yourself. Consistent revenue keeps your business stable and provides the momentum you need to grow your business to the next level.

You've already seen how getting to revenue as quickly as possible is key to your business success. Early revenue confirms your business model, proving that people are willing to pay for what you offer. It's like getting that first "like" on your first social media business post—it boosts your confidence and shows you're on the right track. Early revenue also covers initial costs and allows you to provide more services. For example, if you're running a lawn care service, your first few paying clients can help you buy equipment or hire additional help, making your service even better.

Setting Your Stretch Goals

You've already earned your first dollars, which is a huge accomplishment. Now it's time to set your next stretch goals. Write down three revenue stretch goals you're going to achieve in the next six months. For example, your first milestone might be earning $700 in the first month, the second could be $1,500 by the end of the third month, and the third might be $3,000 by the end of the sixth month. Use the Google Docs SMART Goal Template you used for your previous goals and place them by your bed.

Bootstrapping

As you've already seen and proven through following the steps in Phase One; bootstrapping is the way to start a business without any money. Most people pour tens and thousands of dollars into their businesses and take years to turn a profit if they even make it past the first year in business. But when you bootstrap, you're using your own resourcefulness to create money out of nothing. It encourages smart spending and quick execution. You learn to make the most of what you have, which often leads to quicker profits and a more sustainable and profitable business model. But generating revenue becomes a priority, as it's the only way to cover expenses and reinvest to grow your business.

One of the key strategies in bootstrapping is structuring your business so that expenses are covered by the revenue generated. This means you need to be very mindful of your spending and focus on activities that bring in income. For example, if you're running a tutoring service, prioritize marketing efforts that attract paying clients (ROI Marketing) rather than spending time and money on fancy business cards or a high-end website. As you increase sales, you have more money to spend on other strategies to grow your business. When you bootstrap, you're conditioned to look at every dollar you spend and see what will have the biggest ROI for you - limited dollars mean you want the biggest bang for your buck to help you with the biggest stair step to grow your business.

When you're working to stabilize your cash flow, you run your business with the minimum needed to provide a quality customer experience. This concept is called MVP for product businesses or Minimum Viable Service (MVS). An MVS is the simplest version of your service that can still deliver value to your customers. Its purpose is to keep costs low and ensure you can get customers and launch and grow your business by generating revenue before you spend money on expanding your services with more equipment, tools, etc. To stick to the minimum and keep an MVS for your business, focus on delivering the minimum amount of work required to attract your first customer and prove your business model. For instance, if you're starting a graphic design service, begin with a basic portfolio and offer a few sample designs to attract your first clients. Emphasize quality, integrity, and speed in executing your MVS to secure initial revenue quickly.

Consider two examples of MVS in action. A teen starting a lawn care business could begin with just a lawnmower and basic tools, offering simple lawn mowing services. They could later expand to include landscaping and garden maintenance as revenue grows. Another example is a teen offering tutoring services. They could start by offering one-on-one sessions in a single subject, then expand to multiple subjects and group sessions as they gain more clients and revenue. These examples show that starting small with an MVS allows you to test your business idea, generate initial revenue, and grow sustainably.

KEY POINTS:

Bootstrapping involves:

- Starting with minimal resources.
- Focusing on smart spending.
- Quickly generating revenue to cover expenses and fuel growth.

Operating with a Minimum Viable Service allows you to test your business idea, secure initial revenue, and expand sustainably.

ACTION STEPS:

Identify the simplest version of your service that can deliver value to customers and focus on delivering it quickly and efficiently to secure your first paying clients.

Credit Cards On File Increase Revenue

Setting your business up to take credit card payments takes almost no effort and has an incredibly high impact. When you take more forms of payment, you can collect more revenue, but once you take credit cards, you shouldn't take Venmo or Paypal anymore, and here's why. One of your biggest advantages for your customers is having a card on file so they can use your services again. Whether you have a monthly subscription service, which we'll talk about later in this Chapter, or a past customer just wants to use your services again, charging their card on file makes it easy to do business with you. We always want to make things easy on your customers so they choose you every time.

One of the easiest ways to take credit cards is to use Stripe. There are no upfront fees or monthly charges to use Stripe; they charge you a fee every time someone uses their credit card, and they take their fees out of the revenue you collect. Start by signing up for a Stripe account on their website. Once you're in, you'll need to link your bank account to receive payments. Stripe also allows you to store customer card information for repeat purchases like we discussed. This is a game-changer because it makes future transactions smoother and faster for your clients. Imagine running a small online tutoring business. With Stripe, you can collect payments in advance for each tutoring session. When a new client signs up, you send them a payment link through Stripe. They pay upfront, and their information is stored for future sessions. This way, you don't have to chase down payments every time and have all your revenue collection data in one place.

This setup saves time and helps you track customer metrics, making it easier to see who your repeat clients are and how much revenue they generate. Because your services are pre-sold, you never have to chase down customers to collect your revenue. Revenue is paid before the service is provided, and if the service is monthly, the client is on a monthly billing plan through Stripe. When you run all of your revenue through Stripe, you can also use their system to identify key business metrics. When you have the key business metrics like how much revenue you make on average per customer or how many times the average customer buys services from you - you can use that information to grow and scale your business to the next level. How much does the average customer pay you for your service? What is their lifetime value?

KEY POINTS:

- Setting up a payment processor like Stripe streamlines your payment process, stores customer information for repeat purchases, and consolidates revenue collection data. Efficient billing practices, such as using payment links and enabling easy input of payment information, ensure timely payments and improve cash flow.

ACTION STEPS:

- Set up a Stripe account and create a payment link for your service. Send this link to your next client to test the system and experience the benefits firsthand.

Getting Paid Every Month Like Clockwork Instead Of Just Once

There are two basic kinds of revenue in a business: transactional and recurring. Let's take the example of a babysitting business. When you get a new customer, and they hire you to babysit their two kids on Friday night from 6pm to 9 pm, and you get paid $20 per hour, you earn $60 from that one customer for that one night. They might call on you again to babysit their kids because you did such a great job, and that would be a transactional customer repurchasing your service. That is excellent because the simple fact that you do such an outstanding job that your customers would come back and pay for your services again is the strongest statement that you have a great business that offers great service. But that business model is transactional.

Let's go back to the goal income of $1,000 a month that we started in this Phase. We understand that in this babysitting business, if you earn $60 on average per customer, you need about 17 monthly customers ($1,000 revenue divided by $60 per average customer) to meet your $1,000 income goal. We also talked about having a 10% sales conversion rate, so in this example, you need 170 leads (17 customers divided by your 10% sales conversion rate) to hit that $1,000 goal. That's only about 6 new leads a day, and that's completely achievable, especially because parents are always looking for great babysitters.

		Leads Per Day	Leads Per Week	Sales Conversion %	New Customers Per Week		
		6	39	10%	4		

Service	Average Babysitting Hours	Hourly Rate	Average Earned Per Babysitting	Revenue Goal	Customers Needed	Leads Needed	Leads Generated Per Day
Babysitting Date Night	3	$20	$60	$1,000	17	167	6

But - there's an incredibly powerful way to make this easier and get to your goal faster every single month. Recurring revenue is the smarter, more efficient, more profitable way to structure your business. In this babysitting example, you can still offer one-time babysitting services and make that $60 from one night with one customer. But - you can offer a recurring plan and ensure that your customer is set up to pay you for your services regularly. In this example, when you're offering your babysitting services to your potential customers, you can talk about the benefits of regular date nights. You also can offer a plan where you set a schedule and have date night twice a month, and instead of your customer paying $60 for each of the two date nights ($120), let's say they save 10% when they sign up for your monthly service and it's only $108 for the month ($120 times 90%).

Average Hours Babysitting	Date Nights Per Month	Average Hourly Rate	Price Per Date Night	Retail Monthly Price
3 hours	2	$20	$60	$120
Monthly Recurring Subscription Discount				10.00%
3 hours	2	$18	$54	$108

Now - you're earning $108 from one customer, and instead of needing 17 customers to hit your $1,000 goal, you only need 10 customers. And instead of needing 170 leads, you only need about 100, about 3 leads per day.

	Leads Per Day	Leads Per Week	Sales Conversion %	New Customers Per Week			
	3	22	10%	3			
Service	Average Babysitting Hours	Hourly Rate	Average Earned Per Babysitting	Revenue Goal	Customers Needed	Leads Needed	Leads Generated Per Day
Subscription	6	$18	$108	$1,000	9	93	3

And the benefits of recurring revenue just keep on coming. Now - instead of starting next month with zero clients on the books and having to get all new customers to reach your $1,000 goal - you are already receiving revenue from the recurring clients that are paying you monthly and love your service and could never imagine life without you. Those customers are also probably telling all of their friends how much better their lives are now that you're giving them 2 date nights a month, giving you even more business through referrals.

Every single business has an opportunity for recurring revenue. The key to recurring revenue is to present the benefits and savings from the beginning, to take the payment information from the beginning, and to set up automatic payment processing through your credit card processor (Stripe) from the beginning. You will definitely have new customers who want to try your services just once before taking advantage of the savings and the convenience that recurring revenue provides them, and there's no problem with that.

You chose a business that you are exceptional at, and you provide an extremely high-quality service. That single fact ensures that your customers will love you; they will come back and repurchase your transactional offers. They are very likely to take you up on a recurring revenue offer because you do such a great job. Other examples of recurring revenue offers include, if you run a tutoring service, you could offer a monthly subscription for weekly sessions. A pet-sitting business could provide regular visits as part of a subscription plan.

Similarly, a lawn care service could offer weekly or bi-weekly maintenance packages. If you're tech-savvy, you could offer local small businesses a monthly IT support service. These recurring offers not only simplify your business model but also build a steady income stream over time, reducing the stress of constantly chasing new customers.

KEY POINTS:

- Transactional revenue involves one-time payments for services, while recurring revenue creates a steady income stream through regular payments, reducing the need to constantly chase new customers.
- Offering recurring plans (such as a monthly babysitting service) helps secure long-term customers, creates predictable income, and reduces the number of new leads needed to meet revenue goals.
- Almost any business—whether babysitting, tutoring, lawn care, or IT support—can create recurring revenue by offering subscription-based services.

ACTION STEPS:

- Develop a monthly or weekly plan for your service, offering convenience and savings for your customers so you have a recurring revenue offer for your business to build consistent cash flow.
- Recurring Revenue Offer Pricing Template
- Pitch the recurring offer as a savings option when setting up a new customer relationship. Even when the customer chooses a one-time service to start, schedule a follow-up in your Google calendar to offer them the recurring service option for additional savings later.
- Set up automatic payments through Stripe to simplify the process for you and your customers.

The Quality of Your Customer Experience is Everything

Imagine you're a parent and just hired a teen to tutor your kid; the first tutoring lesson is this week. You signed up with this teen a week ago, paid him, and never got any info via email or text, and haven't heard from him since. It's 10 minutes after the scheduled time that he was supposed to be here, and you still haven't heard from him. What is your impression of this teen so far?

If you were to think of a few adjectives to describe your experience so far - what would those be? Now imagine this same example of hiring a teen to tutor your kid, but imagine that after the phone call where you paid the teen, you got a text and an email with a calendar event that included a summary of the services, and you know exactly what to expect. You got a text last night confirming today's tutoring session, and he showed up 5 minutes early for the scheduled time just to introduce himself to you and your kid and get set up for the first session. Now - what is your impression of the service? What adjectives would you use to describe this experience as the parent and new customer?

Pro tip - when you schedule the services for your customers after they complete payment, schedule the appointment in your Google calendar tied to your business Gmail to stay organized and professional. Add your customer's email as an attendee to the event, and schedule a reminder to go out to them 1 day before and 1 hour before automatically. Then, paste your summary of services in the notes/details section of the Google calendar event. This is an easy way to stay organized and show a high level of professionalism and organization to your customers. You can even set the events as recurring in your calendar and use the same system to schedule your recurring appointments when your customer signs up for your recurring revenue services.

The quality of your customer experience can be the difference between a one-time client and a loyal, long-term customer. It can also be the difference between a good review and someone who refers you a bunch of new customers versus a bad review and someone telling everyone they know to stay away from you and your business. When you under-promise and over-deliver and just do what you say you're doing to do, you place yourself ahead of 99% of your competition.

Making sure you are communicating early and often, setting proper expectations, and showing up early to appointments; these simple things establish trust and credibility and are invaluable. Just like the basics of being a great salesperson are the basics of being a great person, the basics of providing excellent service are also the basics of being a person of your word. These basic qualities are important across every area of your life and absolutely set you up for success as a business owner.

Excellent customer service not only helps in retaining customers but also builds loyalty. 89% of consumers are more likely to make another purchase after a positive customer service experience (Source 2). A single good experience can turn a one-time client into a repeat customer. Moreover, 68% of consumers are willing to pay more for products and services from a brand known for good customer service (Source 2). This means that your investment in customer service can even justify higher prices for your services.

Costco and Nordstrom are two companies that have established a superior customer service brand in very different ways. When there's a choice to purchase something at a competitor or to purchase from Costco or Nordstrom, customers will choose to buy there because they know they'll be taken care of; even when the price is a little bit higher than the competition, customers will pay for the trusted brand to ensure they have a great customer experience.

Creating raving fans out of your existing customers takes much less time, money, and effort than constantly looking for new customers. Look at it this way: finding new customers requires marketing, outreach, and often discounts or promotions to attract them. In comparison, keeping an existing client happy increases the probability of that client repurchasing your service or signing up for one of your recurring revenue offers with minimal additional effort. Increasing the number of customers that stay with you and continue to purchase your service by just 5% can increase your profits by 25% to 95% (Source 2). In so many areas of your business and your life, small steps create big gains, which is definitely one of them. Making sure you focus on providing excellent customer service can pay you back in increased revenue and profitability for years to come.

KEY POINTS:

- Simple actions like sending confirmations and reminders through Google calendar, showing up early, and setting clear expectations with your customers make all the difference to your customers.
- Exceptional customer service can be the difference between a one-time client and a repeat customer, leading to referrals and positive reviews that fuel your business growth.
- Underpromising and overdelivering set you apart from the competition. Consistently following through on your word leads to better customer satisfaction and loyalty.

ACTION STEPS:

- After receiving payment, create a Google calendar event with your customer's details, including reminders and a summary of services. This keeps both you and your customer organized and informed.
- Send automatic reminders before appointments, confirm details with your clients, and arrive early. This shows you are professional, reliable, and value your customer's time.

Trusted Referrals Are The Easiest Sales

When your friend tells you about a great movie they saw or a great meal they had at a certain restaurant, how much more likely are you to see that movie or try that same meal that they can't stop talking about? That's the power of a trusted referral. Now - let's say you're planning a date and looking for a restaurant to really impress your date - how much more likely are you to go to that same restaurant that your friend recommended? The probability that you're going to go to that same restaurant increased dramatically. When your prospective customers are literally looking for the service you're offering - they will take a trusted referral from a friend, and most times, they'll just go to that referral; they won't even look at any competitors - because they trust their friend and that they want a good service.

Let's say you're running that same babysitting service, and you get a new customer that has two kids that are 4 and 2 years old, and they've never had a date night. You babysit for their date night, and the kids fall in love with you. The parents sign up for your monthly date night babysitting twice a month, and their whole lives are changed because they have started using your service. All of a sudden, they tell their other parents with kids the same age how much they trust you, how their kids love you, and how they're not losing their minds anymore because they have two date nights a month. All of a sudden, you start getting texts and calls from their friends asking about your schedule and if you can fit them in for date night babysitting, too. That is the power of referrals.

Referrals are one of the easiest, most powerful, and, ironically, most cost-effective ways to acquire new customers. Studies show that referral marketing can generate three to five times higher conversion rates than any other method. What's great is that referral marketing is built into the exact process we showed you from the beginning. When you respond to posts online for people asking for a babysitter, for instance, all of a sudden, as you grow, your best customers see that you responded. They refer and respond in the comments right below you to give their stamp of approval on your service. Even when your past customers don't know the new customers asking about your service, the fact that they're recommending and confirming how great you are online becomes your social proof and increases the probability that new customers will trust and sign up for your service.

Referrals have a higher closing percentage because they have a built-in trust factor. When someone recommends your service, the new customer already has a positive impression of you. Now, referrals are typically out of your control as you can't make a past client take the time to refer you. All you can do is encourage and hope they come through, and the better job you do, the more you will see referrals come through. Referrals are never your main source of new customers; your main source of customers is always the strategy that we taught you, where you intentionally seek out new leads in the market for your services and track your sales conversion metrics. Now, you are in full control of hitting your revenue goals each month. Referrals are an incredible bonus that is like an unexpected gift along the way to your goal.

There are a number of ways to encourage your existing, happy customers to refer you to their friends. You can create a referral offer and say when you refer someone who becomes a client, we give them 10% off and you 10% off as a thank you for referring them! This can be a text message you send out to your existing customers once a month to encourage them and give them an opportunity to refer you. You can also add this referral offer to the bottom of every summary of services you send your customers when they sign up with you. Some people are super referrers; they can't stop referring people; it's like breathing; they automatically refer, and it has nothing to do with you.

Some people never refer, no matter how much you encourage them; it's just not in their nature. Most people live somewhere in between those two extremes. So if you respectfully and gently remind people from time to time with a small discount and a word of encouragement and appreciation, they'll likely use that opportunity to send your information to a friend they know who's looking for your services and generate a referral for you. The easiest way to set this up is to utilize promo codes within your Stripe account.

KEY POINTS:

- When someone refers your service to a friend, the new customer already trusts you based on that recommendation. This makes referrals one of the easiest ways to get new clients.
- Referrals typically have a much higher conversion rate than other lead generation methods because of the built-in trust factor.
- Offering incentives like discounts to both the referrer and the new customer is a simple and effective way to encourage more referrals.

ACTION STEPS:

- Use promo codes so both the referrer and the new customer receive a discount, like 10% off, to encourage more word-of-mouth marketing.
- Send a monthly reminder to your existing customers, gently encouraging them to refer to your services and reminding them of the discount.
- Add a referral offer to your service summaries, ensuring customers are consistently reminded that they can earn discounts for sharing your business with others.

Reviews and How They Affected By Your Decisions

The same behavior typically applies to reviews as well; some never take the time to give reviews, and some people always review, but most land somewhere in the middle. One of the easiest things you can implement into your customer service experience is to send a text after a customer appointment where you provided service and ask them for feedback. Let's say you run a house cleaning service, and after you clean the house, you can say, "Thank you for using [business name] today; we would appreciate your feedback on our service today. Have a great day!" Again, it shows incredible professionalism in your business.

You can use any positive feedback as a review for your business and post screenshots of your customers loving your service on social media. If they have any negative feedback, you can learn right away, on the same day of the service, and make any adjustments you need to make sure the customer is happy. Whether it's a miscommunication or an unintentional mistake you made, your customer will watch and see how you handle negative feedback. You have a very small window to turn negative feedback into a very positive experience. Here's an example: Our meal delivery business has delivery drivers who drop off the food. We have these texts sent out every time we have a customer receive meal delivery, and unintentionally, there was a spill of one of the sauces in the bag, and the customer was disappointed. Because we sent a text asking for feedback, they let us know what happened. Immediately, we apologized for the inconvenience, delivered a replacement for what had spilled, and gave them a larger quantity than they had received initially. This turns an unintentional negative experience into an overwhelming positive experience. If it's within your ability to correct the issue, do it immediately. If not, you can always offer a free service or a discount on their next service.

Make sure, no matter what, the customer feels like you went above and beyond to take care of their needs. That's the way you create raving fans. It doesn't matter if the issue was created by your mistake, by a miscommunication, or by something completely out of your control - what matters is that you're the business owner. It's up to you to take responsibility and do whatever it takes to make that customer happy at that moment right now. The actions you take at that moment make all the difference in the world between a raving fan for your business and a person so dissatisfied that they make it their mission to keep others away from your business by posting bad reviews everywhere. Like everything in life, if you just operate in honesty, integrity, and kindness and do the right thing, it literally pays off by supporting the growth of your successful and profitable business.

KEY POINTS:

- Asking for feedback immediately after providing a service shows professionalism and gives you a chance to turn positive feedback into reviews or handle any negative feedback right away.
- Address complaints immediately, even if they're small issues. How you handle negative feedback can turn an unhappy customer into a loyal one.
- Consistently following up and addressing concerns builds trust, and customers who feel valued are more likely to leave positive reviews and recommend your services.

ACTION STEPS:

- Create a simple, professional text message thanking the customer and asking for their feedback, ensuring every client has an opportunity to provide input.
- Use screenshots of positive feedback on your social media to showcase customer satisfaction and build trust with potential clients.

EIGHT

Calculating Profit Margins

I t's actually really easy to create a million-dollar business, but most people do it by spending a million dollars and honestly have no profitability to show for all of that work. That is the last thing you want to do for your business. Some people believe you have to work for months and years in a business before it can be profitable. That is not true. You can be profitable in your business from the very first month; it all depends on how you design it. Each step is strategically laid out for you in this book to create money from nothing and to make sure that you're profitable. You are creating this business to have a monthly income stream for you and your financial benefit for years to come. How you design a business determines whether or not you'll have that income stream for yourself as the owner. Your income stream as the owner is dependent on your business being profitable. In the simplest explanation, Revenue is the money you collect from customers, expenses are the cost for you to provide the service (ideally the very minimum for you to deliver a high-quality service), and the profit is what's left over.

Simplifying Business Expenses

The vast majority of adults don't like to look at their business numbers, avoid them, and don't understand them, which can literally kill their business. Understanding your business numbers is simple and incredibly powerful. We will show you how simple your business expenses are for your new business and how to track them on a simple Google Spreadsheet.

For this example, let's say your business provides graphic design services to local business owners. As always, we want you to provide the highest quality service for the lowest possible cost. In this example, you offer services to design logos, business cards, brochures, social media content, flyers, and other print materials. We covered several steps in Phase One and Phase Two, and here's where we go over those steps to explain expenses.

There are expenses you must pay monthly, no matter what, just to run your business. Those expenses are usually fixed because they're the same monthly price, and we teach you to set those up after you earn your first dollars.

In this graphic design business example, let's say you get your first customer, and after they pay you, you want to use the pro version of Canva for your design service. You pay for that expense out of the customer revenue you collected. That $14.95 expense for Canva is a fixed expense every single month. Whether you do 100 or just one design, it's still $14.95 for the pro version. This doesn't even take into consideration that a lot of the software services have a free trial to start, but do not sign up for the free trial until you have secured payment from your first customer.

Now, let's say that as you grow in your design service, you follow the steps here in Phase Two for Stabilize and set up credit card processing so you can accept credit card payments from your clients using Stripe. Stripe doesn't have a monthly fee; they charge you a fee every time you use them to accept credit cards, so that's a variable expense. If you have one credit card you're taking as payment from one client, they charge you once; if you have 100 credit cards you're taking as payment from 100 clients, they charge you 100 times. Again, some might be tempted to save a few dollars by using Venmo or Paypal to collect payment from your clients - do not do this. There is a very famous saying that says, "Penny wise and pound foolish." It means you miss the big money when trying to save a couple of pennies. The benefit you get from taking credit card payments for recurring revenue and for a much larger amount of customers far outweighs the cost you pay for taking credit cards. If you want to create a real business with real revenue and income generated every month - do not take payment except through your credit card processing company.

Even though you are doing the work yourself, you always have to count the staff expense to ensure you're charging enough and your profitability is safe. As you grow your business, you will end up having more customers than you can handle, so you have to make sure you have enough money to pay other people to do the work for you, even if you're the only one doing the work now. So, let's say you create 4 pieces of social media content for each business owner each month, which takes you maybe 90 minutes of work per customer. Now, you can likely hire someone for about $25 an hour (we'll walk through the steps in Phase Three, Scaling). So, let's say each customer costs you about $37.50 in staff expenses ($25 an hour for approximately 1.5 hours each month).

THE LAST TYPE of expense is just a one-time expense in your business. For example, you purchased your domain name for your business early on, so you could later use that as you grow your business and scale. That one-time expense (even though it's charged annually to renew) was under $20. You don't pay that monthly (fixed overhead expense), and you don't pay that every time you sell your service to a client (variable expense); it's a one-time expense.

Understanding how expenses work allows you to ensure your business is profitable. If you have too many expenses, regardless of the expense type, nothing will be left over.

One of the most important things to remember is that you're creating this business to provide an income stream for your personal financial future. So, when you're running the numbers to ensure your business is profitable, you always want to remember to count how much you will pay yourself personally for the business. If you want $400 a month and you're not making enough to pay yourself that amount- you need to focus on generating more sales. If you want $2,500 a month in personal income, again, you have to calculate how many leads and sales generate that much revenue so you can know exactly what you need to do to pay yourself that much.

In the graphic design business, let's go through the math to earn $1,000 a month in revenue, which was our example in this entire Phase, and then see how much profitability that leaves for your income. When mapping out our plan, we're assuming that we will hit our target and achieve the revenue we set for our goal. In this example, your recurring revenue offer is $100 per month for social media graphics for small business owners. You offer transactional items as well, but we're going to just stick to the recurring revenue offer to keep things easy. Your revenue goal is $1,000 this month. Your average monthly revenue per customer is $100. You need 10 customers to hit your revenue goal ($1,000 revenue divided by $100 service price). Your sales conversion ratio is 10%, so you will need to generate 100 leads (10 clients divided by 10% sales conversion ratio), which is only about 3 new leads a day and is really achievable. Now, let's walk through all your expenses to run this business and make $1,000 a month.

Month One In Business:

One-time expense:

Domain name: $20

Fixed expense:

Canva Pro: $14.95 per month

Variable expense:

Stripe fees: 3% (approximately)

Staff expense: $375 per month ($25 per hour times 1.5 hours per client times 10 clients)

Every other business tool we shared with you is free. There are additional tools you can implement to grow your business, and we'll cover them in Phase Three, where we discuss Scaling your business. But remember—the point isn't to create a bunch of expenses—the entire point is to do the very minimum to create the highest-quality service to make the most profitable business.

So, let's say you collected $1,000 in revenue because you followed all the steps to hit your revenue goal. Let's break down your profitability:

Revenue:				
	$1,000.00			
Expenses:				
	-$20.00	Domain Name		
	-$14.95	Canva Pro		
	-$30.00	Stripe	3%	(Approx. 3% * $1,000 Revenue)
	-$375.00	Staff Expense	$25.00	1.5	10
Total Expenses:	-$439.95		Staff Hourly	Hours Per Client	# Customers
			($25 per hour * (1.5 hours per client * 10 customers)
Gross Profit:	$560.05			
Gross Profit Margin	56%			
Owner Compensation:	$400			
Net Profit:	$160.05			

You get your profit margin when you divide your profitability over your revenue collected.

$560.05 divided by $1,000 equals a gross profit margin of about 56%. Anyone will tell you that a 56% profit margin is a very healthy margin for a service business. Now, at this point, you're pocketing the $375 a month in staff expenses because your customer count is manageable, and you have enough time to provide high-quality service to all your clients.

But it's very important that you also pay yourself $400 per month as owner compensation. You are not only the graphic designer serving the clients; you also own and run the business, and you need to be compensated for that.

So, out of the $560.05 in gross profit, you will pay yourself the $400 as the owner, and you have $160.05 net profit remaining. Transfer that amount into your business savings account. As you see that savings balance grows every month, it's incredible to know that you built that cash balance and have what you need to take advantage of opportunities to grow your business. This is another key way to set you and your business up for success. Managing your cash flow is a key element of managing your business. Understanding how the money comes in and where it goes out, being in control of that cash flow, and knowing how to make moves to directly increase it is the sign of a great business owner. Schedule 2 days a month (usually the 15th and the 30th) for a 30-minute time block to review your cash flow, pay your bills, pay yourself, and transfer your net profit to your business savings account.

Profit margins vary depending on the type of business you run. For instance, restaurants have a very low profit margin but serve a tremendous number of customers; those businesses have high volume and low margins. A high-end diamond jeweler, for instance, has a huge profit margin but might have a much lower volume of customers, so those businesses are low-volume, high-margin. A service business usually has a higher profit margin than a product business; anywhere from 20 - 40% is a good range. As you grow and gain more customers, your expenses will grow, you'll need to hire staff to serve your customers and ensure the quality of your service remains high, you'll need more software to run your business effectively, etc. Keep in mind that every step along the way, you add an expense only if it will help you increase your revenue overall and ensure the growth of your business. By safeguarding your profitability and ensuring your numbers are solid, you continue to set yourself up for success.

Notice that we made sure your personal income was paid out even though your business is new. Many people run their businesses and just hope for something to be left over at the end so they can make some money. That's not setting yourself up for success. You have to make sure the numbers work and there is enough money to pay yourself an appropriate amount so your business is set up to support you and your goals. If the example above only shows that you'll be making $400 per month and you want to make $1,200 a month, then you just need to triple the numbers in leads and sales to hit your personal income amount.

We will cover later how you can leverage your personal income to set yourself up for your own financial future. There was approximately $160 left after paying all of your business expenses and paying yourself. That money is meant to be left there and to grow every month for a very specific reason. When you create cash in your business, you have options for growth. You always want to set yourself up with options in life, so when an opportunity comes your way, and you can get a high ROI on that opportunity, you have the means to be able to take advantage of that opportunity. You don't need any money to start making money in your business, but you can use that skill set to build cash in your business account and give yourself every opportunity to grow.

Here are additional examples of various expenses you might choose to utilize as you grow. Remember, you always want to operate with a mindset of spending money on things that will help you make more money, spending where you will receive the highest ROI.

For example, as you grow in your tutoring business, you might take out a membership in a co-working office to use their office space for tutoring for a very small cost. That would be a fixed expense, and one reason to do that would be if you were going to implement group sessions into your tutoring business and grow your revenue with that service that needs a dedicated space. First, you would pre-sell the group tutoring sessions and ensure you received the pre-payment. You would use those dollars to find a co-working space with availability at a reasonable rate, and that monthly expense would be an additional fixed expense that generated a large ROI with a new revenue-generating service for your business.

Variable expenses, remember, vary depending on how many customers you're serving. Let's say you offer handyman services, and the Holiday season is coming, and you've hung the holiday lights on your own house for your family for years. You know how to do it well to do it safely, and you know how many lights you need based on the house size. You would start pre-selling the service to hang Holiday lights in October because early bird people start hanging their lights in November, and late bird people procrastinate and still do it in December. You would factor the cost of the lights into the service because you would also have to provide the lights each time you do the service. That's a variable expense. You would also likely want a helper to hang the lights with you so you can do a great job, and it takes less time for you and your customers. You need to pay that other person hourly (maybe $25 per hour for 3 hours per house, on average) and factor that expense into your pricing so you're still making a profit on that service.

Let's say you pre-sell more people than you could possibly do - you could bring on even more people and pay them to do the jobs, and you would just manage the quality and ensure the job is done well. This is the first step to scaling your business. Growing the volume of customers you're serving, having great people do the work for you, managing the quality of the service, and running the business overall to even greater revenue numbers. This only works if you correctly factor in the cost of the staff you have providing the service to ensure your business is still profitable. Some people charge far too low and either lose money or don't pay their people well enough, resulting in their business going under. They receive bad reviews from clients as a result of bad work from underpaid staff. Remember - quality always costs less in the long run. When you hire someone, pay them well for their good work and take good care of them. Good staff are worth their weight in gold. Taking care of your staff well is like taking care of your customers well. Again, operating in honesty and integrity, doing the right thing, and just being a good person shines through in every aspect of your business and literally is the difference between a healthy, profitable business and a business that goes up in flames.

One-time expenses are costs that occur occasionally but can sometimes be significant. Let's say you're running your graphic design business, and your whole business is on your computer. You've been using your parents' old computer because you started this business correctly, without spending any money. You're at the point where you definitely need a new computer because your hard drive is full, and you need a new computer to keep providing a quality service to your customers. This expense is not a "nice to have" expense; it's a "need to have" expense to maintain the quality of your customer service. You've grown the revenue to $4,000 a month, and you've been saving the extra profit every month, and you have a healthy cash balance in your business account. Black Friday is coming up, and you'll get a highly discounted holiday price on a great computer for your business, and you'll still have a good amount of cash left in your account after the expense. This is a necessary one-time expense, and you have the money to make the purchase and still have more cash in your account. While these expenses don't happen regularly, they can take a big chunk of your budget. They can happen unexpectedly, so leave the profitability in your account and have it stack every month so you always have options for yourself and your business to make sure you can move forward, no matter what unexpected circumstances arise.

Walking through all of the steps of your business expense and simplification, you might be wondering why so many adults ignore their business expenses or say they don't understand them. The simple answer is that they overcomplicate the process. You want to organize your expenses in a Google Spreadsheet, and every time you add something to your business or as a service, list it on your spreadsheet so it's easy for you to know your profits and expenses. Later, we'll talk about leveraging good business support through a bookkeeper, a tax advisor, a financial planner, etc. But as long as you set your business up with these simple structures and spreadsheets, you'll remain ahead of the game and set up for success.

KEY POINTS:

- Setting up your business to be profitable from the beginning is the difference maker. Tracking your business metrics sets you up for success.
- Fixed expenses are constant costs like rent and utilities, while variable expenses, such as customer materials and labor, fluctuate based on your business activity.
- Knowing how many sales you need to hit your revenue goals and safeguarding your profitability from the beginning ensures you can pay yourself and grow your business effectively.
- Keeping extra cash from your profits allows you to invest in tools or resources when needed, ensuring you can continue to grow your business without being blindsided by unexpected needs.

ACTION STEPS:

- Create a Google calendar event twice a month for 30 minutes to update and review your business numbers. Transfer your owners' pay into your personal bank account as income and your net profit into your business savings account to start stacking.
- Map out all your numbers and update consistently to set yourself up for success using the below template.
- Revenue & Business Metrics Tracking

WIN:

**YOU ARE NOW RECEIVING
STEADY, CONSISTENT DOLLARS
EVERY MONTH IN YOUR BUSINESS.**

Post your win, celebrate, and enjoy your reward.

You should be incredibly proud of yourself.

And you're just getting started.

Inspire Those Looking To Follow with Your Review

Unlock the Power of Leading By Example

"When you share your success, you inspire others to reach for their own."

At this point, you have a huge list of the wins you've accomplished, you've not only acquired your first customer, you're receiving consistent cash flow every single month, which is an enormous accomplishment. You posting your success can be the difference maker for another teen to believe they can achieve similar wins.

Take a minute to help inspire the next teen to follow their dreams and take that big step toward becoming a business owner... and don't forget to share your wins so we can celebrate you.

Remember - I read every single one of the reviews that get posted, and when you share your wins, post pictures or videos about your wins and your takeaways from this book, I get to see and celebrate with you.

Some wins make you feel like you want to cheer and scream at the top of your lungs because you're so incredibly proud of your accomplishment. I totally get it - I still feel that way about my wins too. Post so we can all celebrate them together. You're an action taker and have accomplished so much - even though you're just getting started... I can't wait to read all about it, and stay updated every step along the way.

Chris Rosenberg

P.S. If you haven't gone to Amazon and posted a quick review yet, go there first and then keep going for the bonus... If you've already posted a review from earlier in the book - go and update it with your wins so people can keep cheering you on!

P.P.S. BONUS: If you'd like to cheat sheet of all the spreadsheet templates and resources listed here, you're welcome to send us an email at wins@meridianpub lishinghouse.com.

Make sure to include your wins so we can celebrate you as well!

Leave a review

PHASE THREE SCALE:

GROW YOUR DOLLARS

Every Business is Scalable

Scaling isn't just about doing more so your business gets bigger. The goal of each Phase and the way to accomplish that goal is very different. You've already shown that you provide great service and have gotten your first customer. You've then shown that you can serve multiple customers multiple times, and your business is thriving with consistent revenue. Now, as the owner, your focus shifts from providing the service to growing the business and maintaining that same quality for your customers.

Many people are very good at providing the service they're in, but they never learned how to run the business parts of their business, and you can see how their business is suffering as a result. The most important key strength in scaling your business is to get really good at delegating and leveraging. This is literally a skill that very few adults learn. Most people say, "If you want something done right, do it yourself." "It's impossible to find good help." These phrases come from people who have not developed the skill of delegation and leverage. It is impossible to run a truly successful, large, and profitable business by literally doing everything yourself.

Every single business is scalable. It's about understanding how to strengthen those legs on your table, getting the right people in charge of those legs, and knowing how to execute effectively for your business. Here's a simple example: some people are star athletes, but they're not great at coaching for several reasons. Maybe they're not great at strategy, don't see the big picture, or don't know how to take a star athlete and coach them to perform at the next level of their game. Running your business, which is exactly what scaling is all about, is like coaching a great team. You're not on the field playing the game, but you're responsible for picking the right players to play on the field, putting them in the right roles, and getting your team to work together for the win. Some players never want to coach; they want to stay on the field until they retire, and that's alright, too. You can have a strong, profitable business from the elements in Phase One and Phase Two in this book. But if you want to take your business to the next level and learn how to coach instead of being a player on the field, keep reading. If you're really focused on scaling your business, you need to, at a minimum, be earning at least $3,000 a month for the last two months; if so, you're in a great position to take that next step. The objective now is to grow your cash flow to create independent income and start building wealth.

As always, you start with the goal. It's impossible to create a roadmap to get to your goal if you haven't clearly defined your goal destination. Do you want a business earning $5,000 a month or $50,000 a month? There is no right or wrong goal, only the right one for you. And honestly, goals change over time. The person you are today will not be who you are a year from now. If you're playing this game of life correctly, you're learning, growing, and evolving, whether you're 14, 24, 44, or 64. We are all meant to learn, grow, and evolve because that's the fun of life. Set your goal based on what you want today, and know that as you grow, you can change and evolve your goal later.

For the purposes of this Section of the book, we're going to set a goal of $10,000 a month in revenue, which represents a business earning $120,000 a year in revenue, which many people refer to as a six-figure business. This goal is completely achievable, no matter your age. Whether you're 16 and reading and executing the steps of this book or a parent who stole this book from your kid, which we totally understand, the principles and steps are the same. As I mentioned, the most recent business we scaled in our own personal family exceeded $10,000 in revenue by its 3rd month in business and exceeded $100,000 in revenue in its 9th month in business. I want you to recognize what it looks like to be on track for six-figure revenue. Let's say within 2 months from now, you have your first month where your revenue exceeds $10,000. That means you're on track if you just do the same thing you're doing for another 11 months to earn six figures in your business. Now, as you already know, when you do things consistently, you get better at them, whether it's creating leads, converting sales, delivering your service, or hiring staff. So inevitably, once you break $10,000 in revenue in your business, you're likely going to keep going up because the more you do things, the better you get at those specific skills. So, just reaching your first $10,000 month is a huge accomplishment because you know you're on track to break six figures in your business over the next 12 months. So now that we have our goal of $10,000 a month in revenue, we can move forward, scale appropriately, and take specific step-by-step action to crush that goal. Every step you've taken so far has literally set you up for this success in your business. Now, it's just about putting the next pieces together. Let's do this.

NINE

Scaling and Managing Growth

Knowing You Win Because You're Just Built Different

I magine you're in your garage, editing photos from your last family photo session for your customers. You literally love everything about this business, you're really good at it, and you're confident that this will be the basis for your six-figure business. Now, picture someone who was once in a similar situation: Elon Musk. Before he became the CEO of Tesla and SpaceX, Musk was often seen as arrogant. His confidence, however, enabled him to push through challenges and turn his visions into reality. He faced numerous setbacks, from nearly going bankrupt to having rockets explode. Yet, his unwavering self-belief kept him moving forward, transforming his ideas into groundbreaking companies.

Self-confidence is a game-changer in the entrepreneurial world. It's the difference between taking action and holding back. Confidence helps you believe in your vision, which is crucial when you're trying to convince others—whether they're customers, investors, or partners. But there's a fine line between confidence and arrogance. Confidence is believing in your abilities and being open to feedback, while arrogance is thinking you're always right and dismissing others' opinions. Studies show that self-confident entrepreneurs are more likely to succeed because they're better at taking risks and pushing through failures (Source 2).

Building self-confidence isn't something that happens overnight, and that skill comes easier to some than others. Utilizing the same strategies that we covered in the beginning sets you up to build these very skills. Building a skill like sales or self-confidence is exactly like building muscles in the gym by working out. The more reps you do, the more your muscles grow. The process is the same for any skill. The more reps you do by pitching your services, the better your muscle (your sales skill) grows. The more wins you write every single day, consistently, in your brag book, the more undeniable your abilities are, which fuels your own self-confidence. But just like anything else - if you go to the gym one time for 5 hours and never go again - how much muscle development will that create? Conversely, if you go to the gym for 20 minutes every single day for a year, how much muscle development will that create? Building muscle - whether it's your business, your sales skill, your lead generation, your spreadsheet abilities, your self-confidence, or whatever it is you want to get great at - it's about building the muscle, developing that new skill set by working at it every single day and then looking back a year later and seeing how much of an impact you've created.

Remember, this whole time, you're supposed to be documenting your wins and enjoying the rewards. Each time you crush a goal, your confidence grows. Each time you enjoy a reward, it feels both exciting and expected, and that's an incredible feeling. Each time you meet with your accountability partner and go over your accomplishments for the week, it's the same - exciting and expected. Keep celebrating these successes, no matter how small they seem. Maybe you landed your first customer on a new recurring revenue service you're offering or successfully turned around a customer who was very upset by a staff member and now is in love with you and your business based on how you quickly and effectively handled the situation. Take the time to acknowledge your hard work and huge accomplishments. The fact that you are achieving what very few adults, and even fewer teens, have accomplished at your age is incredible. And know that you're just getting started, and things just keep getting better and better.

Another pro tip is to make sure that your social media feed is feeding you things to help you with your mindset and your goals, not the opposite. Take 15 minutes and make sure that the people you're connected to on Facebook and the accounts you follow on Instagram (or YouTube or TikTok) are inspirational, motivational, and educational. Your vibe goes up when you see those posts. When part of your strategy to get new customers requires you to spend time on social media, it's even more important that you make sure that the feed you have is bringing you up and setting you up for good vibes instead of being distracted or brought down. Unfollow any accounts that bring you down or cause you to go down the rabbit hole of social media. Follow motivational business accounts, young entrepreneurs, and inspirational figures. Seeing their quotes and successes can motivate you and provide a random pick-me-up you didn't even know you needed. Let's say you're starting a small landscaping business. Follow accounts of successful gardeners, landscapers, and entrepreneurs. Their stories and tips can be incredibly motivating and help give you ideas that you can implement for your own business and customers.

KEY POINTS:

- Believing in yourself and your abilities is essential for overcoming challenges, taking risks, and achieving your goals—just like every single entrepreneur who's come before you and everyone who will come after you.
- Just like building muscles, you develop confidence and skills by working at them every day. The more you practice, whether it's sales, customer service, or any other aspect of your business, the stronger you'll become.

- Ensure your social media feed is full of content that raises your vibe and motivates and inspires you towards achieving your goals.
- Self-confidence significantly impacts your entrepreneurial success. It helps you take risks, push through challenges, and take action to make your vision a reality. Setting and achieving small goals, celebrating wins, and living your 2.0 life today all work to set you up for success.

ACTION STEPS:

- Keep track of your wins, no matter how small, in your brag book. This will build your muscle and always remind you of how far you've come when you need to raise your vibe.
- Be an example for others. Post your wins, as we mentioned after the Launch Phase. We'll remind you again after this Phase. You are the living, breathing example for the next teen who wants to come up. Your wins are their inspiration, and they can make them believe that they can achieve what you have achieved.
- Unfollow accounts that don't raise your vibe. In life, you progress, or you regress; there is no such thing as standing still. The same goes for your feed—what you're watching is either raising your vibe or dropping it. Notice the difference and adjust accordingly. Follow motivational and entrepreneurial accounts that help elevate your mindset and motivate you to reach your goals.

The Exact Roadmap To Your Scaling Goal

You know what's coming next - let's map out exactly how to get you to your $10,000 a-month revenue goal. That's the beauty of understanding this kind of business math, which is called Revenue Projections. You now know exactly how to map out how to get to any one of your business goals. This time, the goal is a little larger and requires providing service to more customers than you can likely take care of on your own, so we're going to be factoring in more staff expenses. Remember, even though we always want to keep our expenses at a minimum, we never do anything to jeopardize the quality of our service to our customers. The quality of service is literally the difference between staying in business or going out of business. Now, let's break down this $10,000 revenue goal. To make it easy, let's stick with this graphic design business that offers social media content for $100 a month to local business customers.

To hit your $10,000 revenue goal, you're going to need 100 customers (10,000 divided by $100 service). Now, you've been offering this service, providing great quality, and keeping your customers happy for months now. Consider if you raise your price to either $125 or $150. How much impact would that create in terms of your revenue growth? You can raise your rate simply because your service is of the highest quality, and you are still offering a great rate compared to your local competitors. Or, you can add more services at the new increased rate. For instance, let's say your $100 rate provided 4 social media posts to the local business, one for each week they'll post. Maybe your new $150 rate includes the 4 social media posts and 1 video reel. Creating a compilation and related video shouldn't take much more time, and the value is significant to the customer. Do not raise your rates on your existing customers; honor the fact that they have been with you from the beginning. If they want to upgrade to the larger package, that's fine, but don't just raise their rates. Now, with the new $150 monthly price, all of a sudden, you only need 67 new clients. That made a significant impact. ($10,000 divided by $150 service).

TO GET your 67 customers with a 20% sales conversion ratio, you'll need 335 new leads. Remember, you've been doing this a while now, and over time, with practice and follow-up, your sales conversion ratio should increase. Make sure you're keeping track of all your numbers so you can use your real averages. See how raising the price of your service and improving your sales conversion skills both have a huge impact on your roadmap to reach your goal? Every piece of the business is structured that way to set you up for your success, both in your profitability and in your growth.

Now, remember a few things here. One, you're not starting from scratch. You're at Phase Three and looking at scaling your business, which means you already have a base of leads, you already have customers that you're serving, and you're already generating a great revenue and income stream on a consistent business. When you set a larger goal, like $10,000 a month in revenue, $50,000 a month in revenue, or $100,000 a month in revenue, they typically aren't achieved within a 30-day period. So, this scaling roadmap is going to be over the course of a few months, but you'll be growing and earning and learning steadily as you follow the path.

Also - one thing we haven't covered yet is customer fallout. When someone signs up for a recurring revenue service with you, whether it's tutoring, date night babysitting, or social media management for a small business, they won't stay with you as a customer forever. This is completely normal and to be expected. This business concept is called customer fallout or churn. A certain number of recurring revenue customers (subscriptions) will discontinue services with you every month, and that's normal and inevitable. It's not necessarily a reflection of you, your service, or your business, but life happens.

Sometimes people's finances change, sometimes their needs or priorities change, sometimes they want to try a different company, and then they come back to you because they realize you provide a better service. Customer fallout is a normal part of any service business. You always check in to see if you can get feedback to see how you can improve as a business. You always check back (unless they unsubscribed from your lists) and continue offering them promotions, etc., and some of those old customers will return to you over time. However, because customer fallout is an inevitable part of business, continuing to bring on new customers is a required part of every business, no matter what size or age your business is.

So, let's break down this $10,000 revenue goal starting today and add an extra $10,000 in revenue from this point on.

Let's start with lead generation. For you to gain $10,000 in new revenue, you need to attract 335 new leads. Now, you've been tracking your lead generation since Phase One Launch, so you should have a good sense of how many leads you can attract each day and how long it takes you. For the purposes of this example, let's say you spend approximately one hour each day (15 minutes to post and maybe 45 minutes spread out to respond to inquiries, follow-up, etc.) doing keyword searches on local social media and responding to posts and inquiries about your service online. It generates about 3 leads each day, and you work 5 days a week on lead generation. That's a total of about 5 hours a week on lead generation. That means that you will create 335 leads in approximately 112 days (335 leads divided by 3 leads a day). That literally means you can reach your $10,000 revenue goal in less than 4 months. How incredible is that?

Now, we're not done here. Let's keep talking this through, as there's only one of you, and you have to make time for all the pieces to work effectively. One of the most important things in your business is revenue generation. So when you're looking to grow, you want to make sure you are still bringing in customers and new revenue, and you bring in more staff to help you provide the service while maintaining the quality.

We discussed how about one hour a day creates the leads.

The way we structured your marketing and lead generation, a lot of the communication is done online or via text. When you speak to a customer, they're asking some final questions, booking your services, and coordinating payment and your calendar availability. Let's say that each time you convert a new customer on the phone, it takes about 30 minutes. Based on your sales conversion ratio, you convert 20% of your leads, so you need 67 new customers to get to your $10,000 revenue goal. So each week you need to bring on about 4 new customers. (4 months divided by 4 weeks equals 16 weeks. 67 customers divided by 16 weeks equals approximately 4 new customers a week. 4 new customers at 30 minutes each takes about 2 hours of your time each week.

Now, where are you going to get the time to provide high-quality service to all of these 67 new customers you're bringing on in the next 4 months, let alone the existing customers you have, that you are committed to providing consistent quality service? So your customers stay with you as long as possible?

That's where the hiring comes in. That's about 7 hours a week between lead generation and sales conversations. You likely have more than 7 hours a week to spend on your business, but let's break down how long it takes you to actually create social media marketing content. Let's say for each client that brings in $150 a month in revenue for you, it takes you maybe two hours of your time to create 4 social media posts and 1 video reel. It might take you more or less time. Let's just make the example simple, and you adjust your real numbers when you calculate this for your business, as always. Now, when you have 67 new clients, and they each need 2 hours for the month, that means that you need to dedicate 134 hours a month (67 clients times 2 hours per client), which equals about 34 hours a week (134 hours per month divided by 4 weeks a month) of working time to deliver your service. That is excellent news.

Here are a couple things to consider. You don't have those 67 new additional clients today. You are bringing on those clients at a rate of about 4 new customers a week. 4 new customers a week create about 8 hours of new work a week that you need to deliver (4 new customers a week times 2 hours of work per customer).

This is how and where you hire your first staff member. You bring someone on to deliver high-quality service at a competitive hourly rate. You start them off by giving them just a few hours of work a week at a time to make sure their quality of work is up to your standard, and you explain to them that as they show you the quality of work they provide, you will continue to give them more hours. You can hire off of either Fiverr or Upwork; we'll walk through the steps of how to hire that person in this section. Let's say this new staff member is paid $25 an hour to create social media content. (You might pay more or less depending on who you choose; we're just creating the example so we can work through the profitability). Now, you have a staff expense of $50 per customer per month. This is a variable expense.

Now, you might think, I can do the work myself and just keep the $50... but how many customers can you really service while running the business, while doing lead gen, while doing sales, etc. You build your business correctly and profitably, and the money is there to hire, and the road is there to hit whatever revenue goal you want to achieve. The point is not to do everything yourself. In life, if you want to go far, you go together. You construct a high-quality team, and you can reach whatever goal and travel whatever distance you want in life. Now, when you look at your profit margins and your calculations like we did in an earlier Chapter, let's update them with this new staff expense:

Revenue:					
	$10,000.00				
Expenses:					
	-$14.95	Canva Pro			
	-$300.00	Stripe	3%	(Approx. 3% * $10,000 Revenue)	
	-$3,350.00	Staff Expense	$25.00	2	67
Total Expenses:	-$3,664.95		Staff Hourly	Hours Per Client	# Customers
			($25 per hour * (2 hours per client * 67 customers)		
Gross Profit:	$6,335.05				
Gross Profit Margin	63%				
Owner Compensation:	$4,000				
Net Profit:	$2,335.05				

Now, when you divide your profitability over your revenue collected, you get your profit margin.

$6,335.05 divided by $10,000 equals a profit margin of about 63%, even with you hiring staff to take care of the delivery of your graphic design service. Now, at $1,000 per month in revenue, you pay yourself $400 each month. At $10,000 in revenue, you're paying yourself $4,000 each month, and you still have cash left over each month. Why? Because you mapped out your numbers to set yourself up for profitability.

$6,335.05 profit - $4,000 owners compensation = $2,335.05 net profit.

As you continue to grow past $10,000 in monthly revenue, you can look at bringing on more support, like a virtual assistant to do admin work or someone to help with lead generation. You can pay for ads to increase leads, but you don't need any of that to get to $10,000. You want to take the straightest path to get to your goal. You already have a proven system, and to get to your $10,000 revenue goal and make another $4,000 a month in your pocket within the next 4 months, this is literally all you need to do. Focus on the task at hand and keep operating at the MVS. Remember - minimum expenses while maintaining quality service to your clients to maximize your ROI and profitability in your business with consistent cash flow.

Expanding your service offerings is one of the ways you can easily increase your average revenue per customer. We discussed earlier in the Stabilize Section that you should consider complementary services that you can offer to your customers to increase your revenue. Remember how increasing your monthly service from $100 to $150 for the graphic design business had a huge impact on how quickly you can achieve your revenue goal. Set a 30-minute block each week to brainstorm and consider which complementary services you can offer to increase the average revenue you get from each client while also meeting the needs of your client. You have to make sure that you can still maintain the highest quality level of service. The last thing you want to do is offer a service that you don't really know how to deliver and lose a client, or worse yet, get bad reviews or a bad reputation just because you wanted to make a few more dollars. Remember, for every service you offer, you have to provide a very high level of quality so you can maintain your customer satisfaction and reputation with your customers.

KEY POINTS:

- Revenue projections help you break down larger income goals into achievable steps. Understanding how many customers and leads you need gives you the exact path to crush your goal, no matter what goal you have your sights on.
- To hit higher revenue targets, consider raising your prices by adding more value to your services. Offering additional content or packages can increase your revenue per customer.
- To hit that next level of growth, you will need to hire staff to maintain the quality of your service while freeing up your time. This allows you to manage lead generation, sales, and business growth more effectively.

ACTION STEPS:

- Break Down Your Revenue Goal by calculating the number of clients, leads, and sales conversions you need to hit your target, adjusting your rates and services to see how these numbers change. Here's the Revenue & Business Metrics Template again.

- Hire a staff member to handle service delivery, starting with just a few hours per week to ensure quality. This will free you to focus on lead generation and growing the business.
- Schedule weekly brainstorming sessions to consider new services that complement what you already offer. These can increase revenue per customer while maintaining the quality of your core service.

Cashing In On The Gold That Lives In Your Lists

One of the other opportunities you have to bring on more customers and generate more revenue is the concept of a down-sell offer. When you offer more services to an existing client, that is called an up-sell. You are selling them more services in addition to what they already bought from you. But every week, you generate more leads, and there is a large percentage of leads that have not yet converted into any kind of customer for you. They reached out and inquired about your services; they said they were in the market for your specific service, they gave you their cell phone number, they receive all of your monthly promotions, and they haven't unsubscribed, so they're obviously still interested, but they haven't converted into a customer.

These prospective customers are unconverted leads. You can create something called a down-sell offer to encourage them to try your services in hopes that they will love what you provide so much that they will continue to purchase your services once they've experienced the quality you provide. For instance, if someone isn't ready to commit to a full landscaping service, offer a smaller, more affordable package like a one-time yard cleanup.

Here's a ChatGPT prompt to help get more down-sell ideas.

"I have a new teen business offering [services] to [target market] in [local area]. My main service is [main service]. Please provide me with 15 down-sell service options."

You can also use this prompt to give you ideas for upsell opportunities.

One of the most important traits that successful business owners have is the ability to focus on the task at hand. The ability to prioritize the work needed to specifically accomplish the goal and not get distracted by random tasks that keep them busy but don't necessarily get them any closer to their goal is key for a business owner. As you scale to crush your $10,000 a-month goal, there are things you can incorporate to help organize and benefit your business that aren't direct revenue drivers but help improve your efficiency, especially when you grow the number of leads and the number of customers you have. When you have 20 or 30 leads, it's very different than managing hundreds or thousands of leads. Remember - these leads are gold. In there lie actual paying customers and real dollars for you and your business.

One of the most beneficial things you can do is shift to a CRM. A CRM is a software system that helps organize your business contacts and communicate with them more efficiently. Before we talk through the benefits of CRM and the reasons why one should be used, a simple upgrade that makes sense at this point is to use

Google Workspace. Up to this point, you've been using a free Gmail account for the name of your business, but since you're about to hire your first staff member and incorporate a CRM to help increase your revenue, setting up Google Workspace brings everything together. Google Workspace is the same as free Gmail, but it's set up so your email is yourname@yourbusinessname.com. You bought your domain in Phase One when you were setting up your Instagram. Go back to your domain provider (name.com or Godaddy.com and set up Google Workspace for your domain name. When you bring on your team members, you'll be giving them an email address through your domain, so it makes sense to set it up now. When you're setting up your CRM, you're going to be connecting it to your Google Workspace email as well. Your domain provider will walk you through the steps to set this up.

Now, back to the benefits of your CRM. The CRM can connect your phone, your texting, your calendar, your notes, your email, and every part of your communication with someone, whether they're a lead or a paying customer. A CRM saves time, increases sales conversion, and improves customer service. One of the simplest CRM systems that's affordable and easy to use is Active Campaign. You can really go down a rabbit hole and lose time and focus when looking at software or setting up software. There can be 1,000 different functionalities and services offered, but here are the basic ones for you to set up and leverage for the biggest impact. In your CRM, you want to set up and connect your email, your texting, and your Stripe account, and you should set up a free calendar booking link through Calendly. This is a huge benefit to you and your customers and can increase your sales conversion dramatically.

When you use a calendar booking link, you add convenience in scheduling for your leads and for your clients. The easier you make the sale, and the easier you make it to book your services, the more sales you will have. You've already been using your business email for your Google calendar, and all of your time blocking and customer appointments are listed. When you connect your work calendar to a booking link, your prospective customer leads can book a call with you to sign up for your service or book their next service with you. Imagine looking at your calendar for the week and seeing that you have 2 new customer services that you didn't even know about because they booked automatically on your calendar. It's like earning money automatically.

Depending on your business, here are a couple different ways to utilize your calendar booking link to increase revenue. Let's say that you're running a pool cleaning service, and you decided to offer a spring promotion for 15% off your service if you book this week. You send your calendar link out with your promotion, and you show that you have availability for new customers on Saturday and Sunday mornings. You sent the text out to your leads, and all of a sudden, two new people booked you for Saturday morning. You sent the text to a list of leads in your CRM, the calendar link is from your CRM, and you collected payment all through your CRM. It's like you clicked a button and made money all in one step.

Now, let's say that you offer tutoring, and parents really prefer to talk with you about their kids before booking. Let's say you offer a back-to-school promotion to start your kids off on the right foot and make sure they stay on track this year. You offer a 20-minute free consultation to discuss the best way to support your kid with a 15% back-to-school promo for tutoring. You click to send the text promo to your lead list with the booking link and no payment option. You have your calendar availability there for sales conversations, and all of a sudden, you booked 3 sales calls for this week straight from clicking the link in your CRM. We haven't even touched on how your CRM can automate follow-ups... remember when we said the fortune is in the follow-up? Imagine being able to set that up and have it run automatically. Whether you're booking sales calls or customer service appointments, the CRM saves time and helps you generate money. It takes a few steps to get set up, but once you set it up for your business, it helps you grow to the next level. It also helps you organize and keep track of the work that's being done for your customers, especially when you're bringing on new team members.

KEY POINTS:

- A down-sell offer gives unconverted leads a lower-priced option to try your services. This allows them to experience the quality of your work without a large commitment, potentially turning them into recurring customers.
- A CRM system makes it easier to manage leads and provide excellent customer service, allowing you to increase revenue with fewer steps.
- Sending out your calendar booking link to your contacts through your CRM allows potential customers to easily schedule services, leading to more bookings without needing to actively manage each appointment.

ACTION STEPS:

- Create a Down-Sell Offer to offer unconverted leads.

  Use a ChatGPT prompt like:

  "What are 15 down-sell service ideas for [your service]?" to brainstorm options.

- Set Up a CRM to manage leads, email, texting, and payment processing in one system. Connect your business email, Stripe account, and texting. Here is the link to set up Active Campaign
- Use a calendar Booking Link: Sending your calendar link makes it easier for leads and customers to book services to save time and increase your chances of closing sales. Here is the link to set up Calendly.

Strategic Partnerships

Remember how we discussed how trusted referrals are like gold and some of the easiest sales you'll ever get? Customer referrals are incredible and come in from time to time, but the frequency of a customer coming across someone who also needs your service can vary. But imagine getting referrals from someone who can refer you almost every single day? That is the power of a strategic partner. A strategic partner is someone who serves your target market with a service that's different than yours but complementary. Let's say that you run a pool cleaning service; a perfect strategic partner for you would be someone who installs or repairs pools. They don't offer pool cleaning, but every single day, they're talking to customers who need a reliable, high-quality pool cleaning service.

The strategic partner always wants to be able to find good, high-quality, reliable referrals because when a customer asks you for a referral, you want to be able to provide it and meet the needs of your customer. If you have a landscaping business, your strategic partner would be a landscaping contractor. If you have a babysitting business, your strategic partners would be preschools. If you run a pet-sitting and pet-walking business, your strategic partners would be local vet offices. Book 30 minutes twice a week to develop strategic partnerships in your local area. Book 30 minutes to use only to reach out and connect with various partners to create a referral partnership. Set a goal for the other 30-minute window each week to be a call or a face-to-face meeting to establish that strategic partnership with that business in your community. Here are a series of Chat GPT prompts to help you build these partnerships in your local area for your specific business.

- ChatGPT prompt to identify your business's strategic partners:

  "I started a teen business for [service] in [local area] serving [target market]. Please provide me with a list of 10 local strategic partners I can reach out to for referrals."

- ChatGPT prompts you to make a list of each of these potential partners in your area with their contact information.

  "Please provide me with 5 local businesses in the [local area] with phone and website information in each of these categories that I can reach out to." Now, take this list and copy it into a spreadsheet to make notes and keep track of how you're reaching out to these potential partners. Each time you're going to reach out, make sure you click on the website and learn about the business for a few minutes so you can address the person intelligently and have the best opportunity to make a connection and schedule a meeting to discuss things further.

- ChatGPT prompt to create an email template and a phone script to reach out to each potential strategic partner:

  "Please provide me with a phone script and an email template that I can use to best connect and partner with these strategic partners in my area to explain how it would benefit their business for them to refer their clients to me for [services]."

After going through this process, you can send emails to the prospective strategic partners using your calendar link to see if you can book a call or an in-person meeting directly with them straight from the email template. You then can follow up with a phone call and reference the email you already sent, looking to meet with them. Ideally, you want to partner with people that want to partner with you as well. You can offer their customers a special discount on your services, like 15% off piano lessons for any referral that comes from the local music shop.

Depending on the partner, they might want a referral fee for sending their clients. You can take the same 15% that you were going to offer as a discount to their clients, keep your standard pricing, and pay that 15% to the music store as a referral fee. However you structure your partnership, always make a promo code specifically for each referral partner to use so the referral is clearly documented by the customer when they're paying for your services. Promo codes are easy to create in Stripe and one of the easiest things to use to track where your sales are coming from.

KEY POINTS:

- While customer referrals can be inconsistent, a strategic partner can regularly send new clients. These partners provide complementary services and share the same target audience, making their referrals highly valuable.
- A successful partnership benefits both businesses. By offering discounts or referral fees to partners, you incentivize them to refer customers and build a strong, lasting relationship.
- Dedicate time weekly to researching and contacting potential strategic partners in your local area. Consistent outreach will help you grow a reliable network that continues to send you new leads.

ACTION STEPS:

- Use ChatGPT to create a list of strategic partners that serve your target audience but offer different services. For example, a pet-sitting business could partner with vet offices, or a babysitting business could partner with preschools.
- Use a template or phone script to introduce yourself to potential partners, explain how partnering can benefit their business, and suggest a meeting. To sweeten the deal, offer special discounts or referral fees.
- Keep a spreadsheet of who you've contacted, their response, and any follow-up actions. Make sure each referral partner has a unique promo code so you can track and reward referrals.

Hiring Your First Employee: What You Need to Know

We have already built out the roadmap to hit your $10,000 revenue goal, the amount of time you need to spend on lead generation, sales calls, and servicing your clients. That roadmap showed us that you are going to have more work than you can handle, and the time to bring on a new team member is now. A lot of people are hesitant to hire; they're worried that they won't have enough work to give that person and that the person won't do a great job. The reality is this - as much as you are dreaming of finding a great person who does high-quality work and is awesome to work with, that person is out there dreaming of you and hoping that they can find the perfect job with the perfect boss. That dream boss is you. You have the opportunity to bring someone on now, train them, make sure the quality of their work is there, and then increase their workload as you bring on more clients. That is a win for you and for your new team member.

Depending on your business, you will either have the option of virtual staff or you will need local staff, depending on whether or not the work needs to be done in person. The process for hiring someone is the same, but where and how you're going to find the right person is going to depend on whether they're virtual or in person. Let's start with virtual. There are websites where you can hire freelancers from all across the world who have the skill set you're looking for and work for a bunch of clients on various projects. Two of those websites are Fiverr and Upwork. Both of those websites have countless candidates that can provide any virtual service you want at very reasonable rates. You can see examples of their work and their experience, read reviews, discuss potential jobs, and even hire them right on the platform. We're going to walk through the steps of picking the right candidate in a minute, but know that once you create an account on the platform, it walks you through the steps to find the right person and get the work done. These sites are a great option for a graphic design business where you're offering social media content creation.

Now, let's say instead that you have a handyman business, and you're going to hang Holiday lights, and you have more clients than you can handle. You need someone local so you can have them help you hang the lights. Or maybe you did so well selling the service that you need to bring on a few two-man crews to get the work done. We're going to turn back to Facebook groups. You're going to create a post saying that you need to hire 1-2 people to help you hang holiday lights for customers. There are always people in your local area looking for work. They need to make extra money; they don't have the skill or the desire to start a business on their own as you did. They just want to show up, do a great job, and get paid the money they need to make. You can help provide an opportunity for those people and for their families. You can post in various Facebook groups that you need to hire, and you can post a simple Google Doc form to get their contact information so you can reach out to them. Now, if it's a virtual candidate, you're going to go to Fiverr or Upwork. If it's a local candidate, you're going to go to Facebook groups and NextDoor. Now, let's talk about the process.

1. The person you want to hire is going to be providing a service that you've already been offering to your customers for months. When you know, you're going to need to hire someone, open up a Google doc and start writing down the exact steps you're taking when you're doing the work for your customers now. When you do something so many times, you almost do it automatically, so when you're training someone new and wanting them to provide service to your client the way you do, you have to map out the steps to make sure they're keeping that quality of service high for your clients. The easiest and quickest way to do that is to take notes in a Google doc the next time you're doing the actual service for a client. Let's say you're doing pool cleaning; map out all the steps you're taking to provide a thorough service and the supplies and/or tools you're using.
2. Once you've taken notes on exactly how you're providing the service to your clients so your new team members can have a good understanding of what you want them to do, keep that information in mind, and we're going to build a job description with ChatGPT.

Here's a basic prompt that you can adjust for your business.

"I run a new teen business for [services], and I need to bring on a new staff member to help me part-time. The position is going to grow over time, but they're going to start out with just a few hours a week, and then they'll get more work each week as they show me the quality of their work. Please write a job description with a few sentences about how awesome our business is, set proper expectations for the opportunity, and list a few basic requirements. The right candidate needs to have these [specific skills]."

1. Now, you're going to make a Google doc TEMPLATE to use as an application form for candidates to submit their applications. You want to do this to be able to reach out and see which candidate is best, but you also want to do this so you can re-use the form next time you need to hire, and in case you want to reach out to these same candidates next time you want to hire. In the Google Docs, you're going to list the job description at the top. When your dream candidate reads this description, you want them to be incredibly excited about the opportunity. You want to sell them on you, your business, and the job, so they can't wait to fill out the application, and they're hoping you call them for an interview. Then, build out the form by asking them the following questions:
    1. Name
    2. Email
    3. Phone Number
    4. Facebook / Instagram / Tiktok link
    5. How many hours a week are you available to work?
    6. How many hours a week do you want to work?
    7. What specific experience do you have for this position?
    8. What interests you most about this position?
    9. How quickly are you available to start work if you're hired?
    10. What is your hourly rate?
    11. Are you flexible based on the right opportunity?
    12. Anything else you want us to consider?

The reason you want to list these questions and let them write out their answers is to get a sense of the person. When someone just writes one-word answers, they don't really care about the opportunity. When you read sentences that someone writes about why they want the job or what they like about the job, you can tell if they're interested, if they're experienced, if they're the kind of person you want to talk to about the job. Do not list the compensation in your job description. Just list the compensation depending on experience. The reason you don't list it is so you can see a range of talent. You might find an awesome person who can do an amazing job for less than you thought you would pay. You might find that the rate you wanted to pay doesn't get you a quality person, and you found the best person ever for $5 more an hour. You ran the numbers, and you can afford to pay more. When you leave the compensation out of the job posting, you have more options. If you listed the lower compensation, that awesome person might never have filled out the application.

Read through all the applications and reach out to the top 3 or 4 candidates you like. Schedule a video call with them using Google Meet from your business email so you can see whether or not they're the right candidate for you. In the Google Meet meeting, explain the opportunity you have, how awesome your business is, and how you have more business than you can handle. Explain how you're looking for someone to start out with just a few hours a week and show you how great of a job they can do, and they would get more work based on the quality you see in their work. Ask them if they feel like the position is a fit for them and why. See whether or not you feel like this is the right person, and let them know that you're interviewing multiple candidates and will get back to them by the end of the week. Confirm that they're good with the compensation that you want to offer them for this position. Confirm that they can start on a timeline that works for you.

Interview all the rest of the candidates and decide who would be the best fit for you. If you have two candidates that are awesome and you're not sure who to choose, or even if you have just one candidate that you want to hire, but you want to make sure the quality of their work is excellent - have them work with you on one job for as a paid trial. Look at your workload this week and identify one piece of client work that you can use as a test to give or do with this new candidate. Let them know that you want them to do one project with you, and you'll pay them based on the compensation you discussed to see if there's a fit. Based on how that one paid project goes, you can let them know if you want them to move forward and join your team.

When you've decided to bring someone on to join your team, they're going to be a contractor. You and they both need to keep track of their hours, and they need to send you an invoice every two weeks listing their hours, the hourly rate you agreed to, and their form of payment. You can either pay them through PayPal or set up a direct bank transfer (for free) from your business checking account. If you're hiring someone virtually, you will pay them directly through Fiverr or Upwork.

Every week, you're going to have a set meeting with them for 30 minutes. You have to manage the hours this person is going to work, especially since you're going to be paying for the hours they work, and you're going to need to manage the quality of their work. In the beginning, you want to make sure to be doing a lot of the work with them so you're training them to provide the same level of quality to your clients that you have been giving this whole time, and your customers are taken care of. This is a very important step in the process. You can have an excellent person with a horrible onboarding and burn the person. It's going to feel like a large investment of your time in the beginning, but it's a key component in the growth of your business. To get more revenue, you need more customers. To get more customers, you need to be able to service them with quality, and you need quality people to help you. You can't expect someone to do what you want, how you want it, if you don't show them. The first step of proper onboarding is for you to do the work and the new team member to watch, then you progress to the new team member doing the work, so you can watch, and then they can graduate to doing the work independently. Managing a team member is all about setting proper expectations and communicating to make sure you stay on the same page. Every week, you're going to have a 1:1 meeting with them to cover the following:

- Review the work they did last week, the hours they spent, and the quality of the work
- Review the specific work you want them to do next week.
- Review how many hours that work will take them, and make sure it's tracked.
- Walk through the work you're giving them and explain how you want it done
- Ask them what support they need to do a great job and what questions they have

Every time you give your team member a new task, you need to map out exactly how you want it done and show them how to do it yourself. A great, free program to do this is through loom.com. Loom can record your screen and your video explaining how to do a specific task. Every time you do something for a client, you can record through loom how to do it so it's a reference video for your new team members to make sure they are set up for success.

KEY POINTS:

- Assess whether it's time to hire by looking at the workload and tasks that can be delegated. Write a clear and compelling job description to attract the right candidates. Recruit and interview effectively by posting job ads on relevant platforms and asking questions that assess skills and cultural fit. Ensure a thorough onboarding process with a checklist and training materials.

ACTION STEPS:

- Take a moment to list the tasks you currently handle in your business. Identify which tasks can be delegated and outline the key responsibilities and qualifications for a new hire. This exercise will help you prepare for the hiring process and ensure you're ready to bring on your first employee.

TEN

Who's In Your Corner

We have discussed solidifying the legs of your table so that you have strong leads, sales, service, and profitability. You're actively working on growing those legs and staffing as needed to support your profitable growth. However, some areas impact your business, your profitability, and your income outside of those areas. Within each of these areas, whether it's tax savings, creating a legal structure like an LLC, or financial planning, there are expert advisors who tailor their recommendations to serve your specific situation and your best interest. In each of these areas, the skill set you need to develop is how to pick the best advisor for you and when to start working with that advisor to set you up for success.

Earning The Most And Paying The Least

One of the benefits of our tax system is that it allows income to be earned to a certain point without having to pay any taxes. This maximum income level changes from year to year, but a quick Google search will tell you the maximum income level this year that you can earn before you have to file for taxes. Now, we recommend that once you start earning around $2,000 a month in gross revenue in your business, you have an initial consultation with a tax advisor. The reason we're saying to wait until you're at about $2,000 a month in revenue is because, until you're at that point, you need to focus solely on revenue generation. Thinking about paying taxes isn't relevant if you're only making a few hundred dollars here or there.

Now, even when you're at the point where you're making $2,000 a month consistently, that doesn't mean that you will necessarily have to pay a significant amount of taxes. When you run a business, you don't pay taxes on your gross revenue. We made sure to create a dedicated checking account and have you keep track of your business on spreadsheets for many reasons, but also because it will benefit you when you speak to a tax advisor. Each of the expenses you incur for your business will reduce the amount of taxes you will have to pay. Every person's financial situation is different depending on the specific area in which they live and how much they earn. So, the next step is to schedule a consultation with a tax advisor.

Ask your parents who they use for a tax advisor and schedule a consultation with their recommendation. When you're choosing an advisor, it's important that you always schedule consultations with at least 2 or 3 providers. You want to sit and have a discussion with that person and see if you're comfortable with them, see if you like their style, and see if they are going to advise you properly and partner with you for your success. You want to make sure that the tax advisor you're scheduling a consultation with has lots of experience with small businesses. If their main client base is all standard employees or large companies, then they don't specialize in your specific type of client. You always want to have an advisor who has expertise that can benefit you in your specific stage of life and business. Within the world of tax advisory, there are countless opportunities to save money and reduce the amount of taxes paid on an annual basis; you want your tax advisor to know which of these strategies would best benefit a new business like yours so you can make sure that you have the best strategic partner to set you up for your success. The tax advisor you choose when your business is earning $2,000 a month might be perfect now, but when you grow your business and you're earning $25,000 a month, you might feel like you need a new advisor, and that's okay. What matters is that you find the best person to advise you now, a person who listens to your goals, recommends strategies that benefit you, and works with you as a partner to educate you on your options so you can make the best decisions for you and your business.

Now, how do you find such a person? Enter Facebook groups again. The way that we taught you to find the best customers looking for your service today is also a very powerful way to get a highly qualified referral for an advisor for you. I would post in your local groups and say, "I have a new teen business offering [services] here in our local community. My business has grown a lot, and I'm looking for a recommendation for a great tax advisor who specializes in small businesses to help me now and as I grow. Any recommendations? Thanks!" The post is structured in this way for a number of reasons. One, people who are interested in your services, even if they don't have a recommendation, will comment and say - I didn't know you have a business offering [services]! I need that! Can you please reach out to me? How much? Etc. So, your recommendation request can literally turn into new customers.

Next, people will be impressed that you're a teen and that you've grown your business to the point where you're looking for a tax advisor. They'll post congratulations and comments celebrating your accomplishment, and they'll even talk about how impressive you are to friends, which can result in referral business for you. You will likely get some posts saying you don't need that; it's too early, don't worry about that. Simply respond to them and say thank you, I'd love to get the recommendation so I can learn more about the next steps as I continue to grow - and leave it at that. Regardless of the comments you get on any of your posts, simply respond respectfully and kindly, and your response will boost your post anyway, so even a less-than-kind comment benefits you. Lastly, you're going to start getting recommendations.

Take note of the different people who are being recommended and who are being recommended multiple times. Check out their website, and schedule a free consultation with the top 2 or 3 people that you like and that you feel like you would work best with. You can have a very talented tax advisor, but they speak to you rudely or condescendingly - that person isn't a great fit. You can have a very kind person, but they don't really have a lot of knowledge or experience. That's not a great fit, either. What matters is that they both have the knowledge and experience, and they're a great partner for you and your personality. When you have these consultations, make sure that you're having the full discussion with the person, and even though your parent is in the room, you are the main person speaking to the tax advisor about your goals, their recommendations for you, asking questions and making a plan to set you up for success.

When you work with a tax advisor, they're going to be giving you advice on how to best track your expenses, which you're already doing on your spreadsheet, and the best plan to keep your taxes as low as possible for you personally and for your business. The costs of setting up a business entity (whether it's an LLC or a Corporation) vary wildly from state to state. In some states, it costs almost nothing; in other states, there are huge annual fees, and you want to make sure to be at a minimum monthly revenue level before you set up a business entity. Your tax advisor will be able to walk you through the benefits and costs, advise you as to when it's in your financial best interest to set up a business entity (to save on taxes, etc.), and they can either do it for you or walk you through the steps to do it yourself.

KEY POINTS:

- You're allowed to earn up to a certain amount without paying taxes.
- Once your business consistently generates around $2,000 a month, consult a tax advisor. They will give you specific advice to help you pay less in taxes, especially as your revenue continues to grow.
- Post in different Facebook groups to get recommendations and find a tax advisor experienced with small businesses. Meet with two to three different people to choose the one that has the experience and is the best personal fit for you and your business.
- Your tax advisor can help you decide when to set up a formal business entity like an LLC or Corporation to potentially help you save even more on taxes. Determining the best timeline depends on your personal situation and the local laws where you live, so discuss with your tax advisor once you choose the best one for you.

ACTION STEPS:

- Once you're earning about $2,000 a month, consult with at least two or three tax advisors to find someone experienced with small businesses who can help you save on taxes and grow your business.

- Post in local Facebook groups to request tax advisor recommendations. This can not only provide you with qualified leads but also generate new customers for your business.

Small Steps Create Big Gains

For years now, my oldest son has sent me videos that he's seen online about how to make money to see whether or not they were real. Many times, they'd talk about a popular concept like real estate or insurance and lay out steps 1, 2, and 10 and say - it's just that easy! But the video would leave out steps 3-9, which were required to actually connect the dots and make the money. So we would talk through those missing steps so he could decide whether or not he wanted to follow the idea inspired by the video as an additional way to make money. But one of those times, he forwarded me a video about the concept of putting away $100 a month, which turned into over a million dollars, and asked whether or not that was real - and I said yes, it absolutely is real. He immediately wanted to put that into action and get started, so that same week, I booked him a consultation with a financial planner so we could put the steps into place.

The reason why putting away a small amount of money today allows you to grow that money into seven figures is due to two different concepts, which we're going to lay out here. The main reason, aside from those concepts, that you can take advantage and make small moves today for big gains is because of your age. Your parents can do the exact same thing and put away the same amount of money as you do each month, but they won't be able to have a balance anywhere near where yours will be because you have the advantage of time on your side.

The first concept that makes this seven-figure reality possible for you is the power of compounding interest, especially over a long period of time. Let's keep this really simple. Let's say you put away $1,000 today, and your savings account pays you 5%. At the end of the year, you would have $1,050. Now, let's say you didn't add any more money to the account after you put away the initial $1,000.

Year 1

Initial Balance $1,000

Interest Rate 5%

Additional deposits 0

Interest Earned $50

Time 1 Year

Ending Balance $1,050

Year 2

Initial Balance $1,050

Interest Rate 5%

Additional deposits 0

Interest Earned $52.50

Time 1 Year

Ending Balance $1,102.50

Now imagine this goes on year after year without ever adding a penny after the initial $1,000 deposit. 25 years later, your Balance would be $3,386.35. Now, you turned $1,000 into over $3,000 just by making a deposit early and letting it grow as you get older. That is the priceless asset you have, just by being your current age.

Initial Balance $1,000

Interest Rate 5%

Additional deposits 0

Time 25 Years

Ending Balance $3,386.35

Now, let's take it one step further and say that you added $100 a month to that initial $1,000 deposit. Now, instead of turning the $1,000 into over $3,000 in 25 years... by depositing as little as $100 a month, which is totally achievable based on the income you have in your business, your Balance in 25 years is now $60.658.87. That is incredible.

Initial Balance $1,000

Interest Rate 5%

Additional deposits of $100 per month

Time 25 Years

Ending Balance $60,658.87

Now, there are a number of variables here within your control.

You get to choose your starting balance.

You get to choose your monthly deposit.

You get to choose how long you're going to leave the money to grow.

The part that you don't get to control is the Interest rate you receive on your money. The interest rate fluctuates depending on the market and the economy overall. In some years, you could get paid less than 1% interest, and in some years, you could get upwards of 5%.

Many people focus on growing a retirement account because there are certain tax benefits you get that don't require you to pay taxes on growth. In this example, you're putting in small amounts of money, and they're turning into much larger amounts of money that could have you paying taxes on those larger amounts of money. One way to make sure you don't have to pay a large amount of taxes is to have the money compound and grow in a retirement account. That is a great discussion to have with your tax advisor, both during your consultation and over time, as your business revenue and your personal income grow. A typical retirement account has a target of 65 years of age, so calculate how many years till you turn 65 and use that as a tool to keep growing your money in this calculation.

Initial Balance $1,000

Interest Rate 5%

Additional deposits of $100 per month

Time 50 Years

Ending Balance $262,684.99

The other concept that makes it achievable to turn a small monthly deposit into a large 7 figure balance is the concept of historical market return. There are a number of ways to invest your money and have that money make you more money. We talk about a number of those strategies in another one of our books, all about Investing, but let's cover one easy concept here. Even though there are a tremendous amount of ways to grow your money, one of them being the business you just built, one of the most common and accessible ways is through investing in stocks and bonds. Now, there are a number of ways to do this, and scheduling your consultation with your financial planner, which we'll discuss in a minute, will set you up to cover the different ways and execute the steps to make it happen.

No matter what, there are ups and downs in the stock market, but one of the most tried and true strategies is to buy and hold. Like many things in life, on a day-to-day basis, things can go up and down, but over a much longer period of time, a year, five years, 15 years, twenty-five years, those things balance out, and overall, there was a tremendous gain. When you look at the top 500 companies in the stock market (S&P 500, which was established in 1957) and look over the course of years from 1957 through 2023, the average annualized return was 10.26%. Now, there were massive losses and massive gains along the way, but when you start early and grow over decades, you get to experience the benefit of long-term gain. So, let's say that we take the same basic calculations we discussed earlier, but instead of using 5% for a savings account, we use a conservative 8% on the historical rate of return on the stock market. Let's run the numbers this way and see what happens.

Initial Balance $1,000

Interest Rate 8%

Additional deposits of $100 per month

Time 50 Years

Ending Balance $735,425.80

Now, you're in control of the deposit amount as well, so let's see how this changes if you go to just $150 per month...

Initial Balance $1,000

Interest Rate 8%

Additional deposits of $100 per month

Time 50 Years

Ending Balance $1,079,687.89

So here are the actual 1 - 10 steps on how to grow a 7-figure bank account by making small steps now. Small steps now create big gains later because time is your greatest advantage because of the power of compounding interest and historical market returns.

Can you absolutely cross the million-dollar mark solely with the growth of your business? Absolutely, you can. But it's not about that. It's about setting yourself up for financial success in multiple ways, including growth in your business revenue and personal income and growth in your financial savings and wealth. Again, there are so many ways to invest and grow your money that we have an entire additional book discussing those options. But the next step for you is to book a consultation with a financial planner so they can go over your specific goals and preferences and custom design the right plan for you and the right steps for you to take today to benefit you for years and years to come.

The moves you make today, setting money aside, doing a full financial consultation with a financial planner, and allowing yourself every advantage to let your money make more money for you, create a payoff that others would dream of but can't touch because they are older than you are right now.

KEY POINTS:

- The earlier you start saving, the more you benefit from compounding interest, which allows your money to grow on itself. Small amounts saved today can lead to significant growth over decades.
- Investing in the stock market over a long period yields consistent growth despite short-term fluctuations. The average annual return for the S&P 500 is 10.26%, which can drastically increase your savings.
- Small Steps Lead to Big Gains. Simple actions, like putting away small monthly amounts, can lead to major financial success when compounded over time. Starting to save early provides an unparalleled advantage.
- Consulting with professionals helps you tailor financial strategies to your individual goals and maximize growth through proper investments and tax benefits.

ACTION STEPS:

- Start Small Now; set aside a small, consistent monthly amount ($100 or more), and watch it grow using compounding interest over time. Use this calculator to play with the numbers yourself.
- Book a Financial Consultation; schedule a meeting with a financial planner to design a custom savings and investment strategy that aligns with your long-term financial goals.

Afterword

You have accomplished more than the vast majority of adults at this point, and you should be incredibly proud of yourself. Whether you began with Phase One at Launch or jumped into Stabilize and Scale, you've set SMART goals, developed your morning routine, monetized your skills and talents, acquired paying customers, and really dialed in your ability to understand your own business metrics. You booked consults with tax advisors and financial planners and created and implemented a plan to set you up for your financial future.

The entire purpose of this book is to serve as a roadmap for you in the growth and execution of your business at every stage of growth. Return to it often and use it as a reference guide. Just like NBA players still practice the fundamentals and attribute their elite status to mastering those fundamentals, day in and day out, it's the same for us as entrepreneurs. Whether it's focusing on getting the highest ROI on your time and money, prioritizing revenue generation, or making sure you're funding the fortune in the follow-up - all of these fundamentals apply from dollar 1 to dollar $1 million in your business.

From mindset to metrics and everything in between, it's the daily practice of living your 2.0 life and prioritizing the most important thing to hit the next goal that will continue to set you up for success. You created money from nothing. You have incredible talents and abilities. You've proven through your execution that you can achieve whatever goal you set your mind to. Continue to follow the roadmap you've designed and executed to the next level of success you want to achieve. But before you go off and crush your next goal, there's just one more thing you need to do. I want to celebrate you and your win as well.

WIN:

YOU HAVE EXCEEDED
$10,000 IN MONTHLY REVENUE
IN YOUR BUSINESS.

THIS PLACES YOU
IN THE TOP 20% OF
SMALL BUSINESSES
ACROSS THE NATION.

You have surpassed
the vast majority of adults
that have begun the process to
Launch, Stabilize and Scale their business.

Post your win, celebrate, and enjoy your reward.

You should be incredibly proud of yourself.

And believe it or not... you're just getting started.

As incredible as your accomplishments
have been to this point...
it just gets better and better...

Keeping the Game Alive

Whether you've launched, stabilized, or scaled your business, it's time to share what you've learned and help others discover the same support you found in this book. I read each and every review posted and celebrate with each and every one of you.

By simply leaving your honest opinion of *Earn Money In Your Teen Business* on Amazon, you'll show other teens who want to build their own businesses where they can find the guidance they're looking for. Your review could be the spark that inspires someone else to take action and follow their passion.

Many teens are looking for the roadmap to start their own path to entrepreneurship, and sharing your wins and your takeaways can be the difference maker for them to choose this same path. Thank you for helping those who are coming after you on this path of teen entrepreneurship. When we pass on our knowledge, we give others the chance to succeed—and you're helping to do just that.

To make a difference, simply scan the QR code below and leave a review:

I also want to celebrate your wins. I read every single one of the reviews that get posted, and when you share your wins, post pictures or videos about your wins and your takeaways from this book, I get to see and celebrate with you.

Some wins make you feel like you want to cheer and scream at the top of your lungs because you're so incredibly proud of your accomplishment. I totally get it - I still feel that way about my wins too. Post so we can all celebrate them together. You're an action taker and have accomplished so much - even though you're just getting started... I can't wait to read all about it, and stay updated every step along the way.

Chris Rosenberg

P.S. If you haven't gone to Amazon and posted a quick review yet, go there first and then keep going for the bonus.... If you've already posted a review from earlier in the book - go and update it with your wins so people can keep cheering you on!

P.P.S. BONUS: If you'd like to cheat sheet of all the spreadsheet templates and resources listed here, you're welcome to send us an email at wins@meridianpub lishinghouse.com. Make sure to include your wins so we can celebrate you as well!

Leave a review

Best Way For A Parent To Support
Their Teen Entrepreneur

Your role as a parent in this entire process is to be your teen's coach. Coaches don't set foot on the field. Coaches encourage and celebrate wins and support and advise when there are challenges and setbacks. You have very specific, high-impact ways to strategically participate in the process. Let's go through those ways now.

Let Your Teen Entrepreneur Lead

The best way for a teen to develop the leadership, decision-making, and problem-solving skills needed for their business and their life is through trial and error. Depending on the nature and personality of your teen, which only you know, they will either race to begin or be hesitant to start. Whichever way they proceed, encourage action and provide advice, but let them be the ones to decide and execute. They will only succeed in their business if they are fully invested and excited in the action they are taking and in control of every part of the process. When they're challenged, have them go back to the direction of the action steps here in the book and ask them questions to help them connect the dots and guide them through discussion, but not in execution. Teens have an incredible advantage in that they are building a business with the support and security of still being at home with their parents. Let them take massive action and feel what both failure and success are like, as they will experience both many, many times on this entrepreneurial journey.

You can offer incredible support by being your teen's accountability partner or helping them find the best accountability partner or mentor for them. Your teen gets to choose who they would best want to partner with, and you get to provide great suggestions based on who you know will support your teen's success most. Do you have someone in your network that would serve as a great mentor?

Someone who has built a business or multiple businesses from scratch? Do you want to build a business yourself? We discuss early on, in the introduction, how you can take these very same principles and step-by-step guidance to build your own business, be an accountability partner for your teen, and make it into a family contest. The shared experiences through building businesses alongside each other, without being partners, but by being accountability partners, are unlike anything you've ever experienced with your teen before. Please note - your teen should not create this business with a partner. They might be tempted, you might even be tempted, to partner with your teen in a business together, but the learning, growth, development, and muscle building that occurs in your teen when launching, stabilizing, and scaling their business alone is unmatched. If they want to do this with a friend, great, have that friend create their own business simultaneously and work in parallel as accountability partners.

When your teen comes to you for help, they inevitably will make sure you reference the material here, as every single step is laid out in order for simple execution to ensure your teen's success. Guide them to get clarity and take the next action. Support and celebrate your teen in every win, small or large. Challenges throughout this process are inevitable, but the way in which they meet the challenge will define their growth and success. Will they shrink back and regress? Or will they rise up, grow, and progress to the next level? This is the same choice adults are given every single day throughout their lives, and our ability to rise up to meet the challenge is what determines our success, time and time again. Challenges are inevitable; growth and ultimate success are choices.

Avoiding the temptation to jump in and do things for your teen will be your biggest key to success as the parent of a teen entrepreneur. Even if you are watching them and you believe, with everything inside of you, that they are making the wrong choice, let them make the choice. Give your opinion, but let them choose. It is only through full autonomy and the ability to decide solely for themselves the best course of action will really develop the business and life skills that you want most for them to possess.

Now, there are key areas where you can level up their success. We already discussed the support in choosing an accountability partner or mentor to benefit them along the way. Early on, we discussed setting up dedicated checking and savings accounts with your teen to separate their finances and make their inevitable tax prep easier. We also want to encourage you to schedule a full consultation with your tax advisor once your teen is earning around $2,000 in monthly revenue in their business. At that point, they will likely have to file their own tax return, and having them sit down and understand how to proactively leverage a tax advisor is invaluable.

You also want to schedule a consultation with a financial advisor early on in the process, as soon as they've earned their first dollars and launched their business. Having a full consultation with a financial planner is mind-blowing to most people, but especially to a teenager. The simple fact that your teenager can put a few dollars away each month and have that turn into millions of dollars down the line will inspire every teen in a way you've never witnessed before. When you're scheduling these consultations with your tax advisor and your financial planner, explain to them that the consultation will be with your teen. You will be in the room, but they will be driving the meeting, providing all the information, and making all the decisions.

During the financial planning meeting, your advisor will likely discuss with your teen their financial goals, their risk tolerance, how much they want to set aside every month to meet their financial goals, and want to set up the accounts to execute that plan. Sit back and let your teen drive this meeting. If you're asked a question, refer back to your teen. You will be completely shocked and impressed by the way your teen responds, their goals for the future, and how aggressively they want to contribute on a monthly basis to be able to reach their personal financial goals. You will likely need to be on their financial accounts as a custodian if your teen is still a minor.

These are the most impactful ways you can support, inspire, and encourage your teen. Let them be the driving force for their own business and their own financial future. Allow them to see the various ways they can take small steps now to leverage the biggest advantage they have to ensure their own financial future, time. After this financial planning consultation meeting, your teen is likely going to want to double down and really grow their business now that they know the financial impact that monthly savings have on their financial future. Encourage them, allow them to capitalize on this momentum, and celebrate every win with them along the way, as it serves to catapult them in their success.

KEY POINTS:

- **Let Your Teen Take the Lead**: Your role as a parent is to coach and support, not to take over. Allow your teen to make decisions, face challenges, and learn from both their successes and failures. This is essential for building their confidence, problem-solving skills, and independence.
- **Be Their Accountability Partner**: Encourage your teen to find an accountability partner or mentor. You can suggest someone, but it's important that they feel comfortable with the choice. Working alongside a mentor or accountability partner will help them stay motivated and on track.
- **Leverage Professional Support**: Schedule consultations with a tax advisor and financial planner when your teen's business starts generating revenue. This will give them a strong understanding of taxes, savings, and financial planning, inspiring them to grow their business while learning invaluable financial literacy.

WIN:

**YOU ARE AN INCREDIBLE PARENT
AND HAVE SUPPORTED YOUR TEEN IN A WAY
FEW OTHER PARENTS EVER HAVE.**

Post your win, celebrate, and enjoy your reward.

The guidance you've given your teen,
and the lessons you have enabled them to learn
and apply are invaluable for their life.

Sometimes being a parent feels thankless...
but you should be incredibly proud of yourself.

Sharing Your Wins Is The Inspiration Others Need

UNLOCK the Power of Leading By Example

"Learning is not just for you; it's a pathway to help others on their journey"

When you take action with your teen and share your success, and your teen's success with others, you make it easier for other parents to follow in your footsteps.

Be the person who makes a difference for the next teen entrepreneur.

Now that you've started your journey with your teen and seen what's possible with *Earn Money In Your Teen Business*, it's time to help someone just like you—someone curious about supporting their teen in starting or scaling their teen business but unsure where to begin.

My mission with this book is to make the process of building a successful, cash-flowing teen business simple and achievable for everyone.

But I need your help to reach more parents who are looking for the right guidance for their teens.

Most people pick their next book based on reviews. So, I'm asking for your help—leave a review and share your wins and your teen's wins.

At this point, you have seen incredible wins from your teen, and in your own journey parenting your entrepreneurial teen.

From your teen's organization or morning routine, to your teen acquiring their first customer, to stabilizing or scaling their cash flow and everything in-between.

As well as your own wins, either in using this resource to create your own business side by side with your teen, or in coaching and guiding your teen through their advisor appointments and all of the life lessons you've witnessed them learning and applying.

You could help inspire another parent make sure their teen has the support to follow their dreams and take that big step toward becoming a business owner.

Your review could help:

- One more parent provide the support their teen has been asking for to start their business.
- One more teen believe they can actually do this because they saw what you were able to accomplish, and that was the difference maker for them.
- One more young entrepreneur start the income stream they need to buy their first house.
- One more teen figure out what they're best at so they can monetize their skills now and know they have what it takes to start a cash-flowing business.
- One more teen start earning now to create their 7-figure reality.

To make a difference, simply scan the QR code below and leave a review:

I also want to celebrate your wins and your teen's wins.

I read every single one of the reviews that get posted, and when you share your wins, post pictures or videos about your wins and your takeaways from this book, I get to see and celebrate with you.

Some wins make you feel like you want to cheer and scream at the top of your lungs because you're so incredibly proud of your accomplishment and your teen's accomplishments.

I totally get it - I still feel that way about my wins too. Post so we can all celebrate them together.

You're an action taker and have accomplished so much - even though you're just getting started... I can't wait to read all about it, and stay updated every step along the way.

Chris Rosenberg

P.S. If you haven't gone to Amazon and posted a quick review yet, go there first and then keep going for the bonus....

If you've already posted a review from earlier in the book - go and update it with your thoughts and wins at this point so you can inspire others and have an even greater impact.

P.P.S. BONUS: If you'd like to cheat sheet of all the spreadsheet templates and resources listed here, for both you and your teen, you're welcome to send us an email at wins@meridianpublishinghouse.com.

Make sure to include your wins and you're teen's wins so we can celebrate you both as well!

References

- American Express. (n.d.). *Revenue in business: What is it and how does it impact profit?* https://www.americanexpress.com/en-us/business/trends-and-insights/articles/revenue-in-business-what-is-it-and-how-does-it-impact-profit/
- Brixx. (n.d.). *Create a financial forecast and plan with ChatGPT*. https://brixx.com/financial-forecasting-and-planning-with-chatgpt/#:~:text=ChatGPT%20can%20help%20by%20analyzing%20historical%20sales%20data%20and%20identifying,the%20coming%20months%20or%20years.
- Bill.com. (n.d.). *12 tips for small business cash flow management*. https://www.bill.com/blog/small-business-cash-flow
- BookingKoala. (n.d.). *How to set up Stripe as your payment processor*. https://help.bookingkoala.com/help/how-to-connect-your-stripe-account
- CareerAddict. (n.d.). *The 15 most successful teen entrepreneurs*. https://www.careeraddict.com/teen-entrepreneurs?srsltid=AfmBOopr1Zn6-MZzp2oR1BIycHJcsvkKTqzV7zJMUJh7r3Cy4VqGFSub
- CardChamp. (n.d.). *Selling is a prerequisite for life & business: How sales skills can impact your success*. https://www.cardchamp.com/blog/selling-is-a-prerequisite-for-life-how-sales-skills-can-impact-your-success#:~:text=Sales%20skills%20are%20essential%20for%20generating%20revenue%2C%20acquiring%20new%20customers,sell%20is%20critical%20for%20success.
- Close. (n.d.). *11 ways to overcome sales call reluctance & build iron confidence*. https://www.close.com/blog/sales-call-reluctance
- D., J. (2021, February 12). *What is the average annual return of the S&P 500?* Investopedia. https://www.investopedia.com/ask/answers/042415/what-average-annual-return-sp-500.asp)
- EasyBooks. (n.d.). *How to calculate expenses in small businesses*. https://www.easybooksapp.com/blog/how-to-calculate-expenses-in-small-businesses)
- Entrepreneur. (n.d.). *The importance of honesty and integrity in business*. https://www.entrepreneur.com/leadership/the-importance-of-honesty-and-integrity-in-business/282957
- Finmark. (n.d.). *How to create a startup budget (template included)*. https://finmark.com/startup-budget/)
- Forbes. (2018, December 21). *5 entrepreneurs on how facing adversity helped them build successful businesses*. https://www.forbes.com/sites/meimeifox/2018/12/21/5-entrepreneurs-on-how-facing-adversity-helped-them-build-successful-businesses/
- Forbes. (2024). *9 business ideas for teens in 2024*. https://www.forbes.com/advisor/business/software/business-ideas-teens/
- Forbes. (2024, July 30). *Parenting tips if your child wants to be an entrepreneur*. https://www.forbes.com/sites/markcperna/2024/07/30/parenting-tips-if-your-child-wants-to-be-an-entrepreneur/
- Forbes Coaches Council. (2022, May 5). *Five business benefits of growth mindset: How to thrive in today's competitive environment*. https://www.forbes.com/councils/forbescoachescouncil/2022/05/05/five-business-benefits-of-growth-mindset-how-to-thrive-in-todays-competitive-environment/
- Forbes Finance Council. (2023, January 12). *Seven finance tips for young entrepreneurs*. https://www.forbes.com/councils/forbesfinancecouncil/2023/01/12/seven-finance-tips-for-young-entrepreneurs/
- From Setbacks to Success. (n.d.). *From setbacks to success: 10 resilient entrepreneurs*. https://beingovee.medium.com/from-setbacks-to-success-10-resilient-entrepreneurs-b829f82c072e
- GoHenry. (n.d.). *24 ways teens can make money online*. https://www.gohenry.com/us/blog/financial-education/24-ways-teens-can-make-money-online
- Greenlight. (n.d.). *6 long term goals for teens to prepare for their future*. https://greenlight.com/learning-center/life-moments-and-milestones/long-term-goals-for-teens)
- Growbo. (n.d.). *Pre-selling simplified: 6 steps to a successful presale*. https://www.growbo.com/pre-selling-guide/
- Guidant Financial. (2023). Small Business Trends Report. https://www.guidantfinancial.com
- Harvard Business School Online. (n.d.). *How to scale a business: 6 tactics to utilize*. https://online.hbs.edu/blog/post/how-to-scale-a-business
- HubSpot. (n.d.). *Overcoming your fear of failure as an entrepreneur*. https://blog.hubspot.com/sales/fear-of-failure

References

- Kaseya. (n.d.). *Recurring revenue: Models, benefits and why it's important*. https://www.kaseya.com/blog/recurring-revenue/
- LeadFuze. (n.d.). *Sales stability: The key to a successful business*. https://www.leadfuze.com/sales-stability/
- LinkedIn. (n.d.). *How to make money as a teenager?* https://www.linkedin.com/pulse/how-make-money-teenager-smartskill97-izkic
- LivePlan. (n.d.). *17 ChatGPT prompts for starting a business in 2024*. https://www.liveplan.com/blog/chatgpt-prompts-for-starting-a-business/
- Nolo. (n.d.). *Hiring your first employee: 13 things you must do*. https://www.nolo.com/legal-encyclopedia/hiring-first-employee-13-things-29463.html
- Oxford Royale. (n.d.). *14 teen entrepreneurs and how they succeeded*. https://www.oxford-royale.com/articles/14-teen-entrepreneurs/
- Problem Solvers Consultants. (n.d.). *Maximize your ROI: Effective paid advertising strategies for small businesses*. https://problemsolversconsultants.com/maximize-your-roi-effective-paid-advertising-strategies-for-small-businesses/
- Rauva. (n.d.). *The importance of continuous learning for entrepreneurs*. https://rauva.com/blog/the-importance-of-continuous-learning-for-entrepreneurs#:~:text=By%20constantly%20improving%20their%20skills,the%20evolving%20needs%20of%20customers.
- Securian Financial. (n.d.). *How does compound interest work?* https://www.securian.com/insights-tools/articles/how-compound-interest-works.html
- Shopify. (n.d.). *11 small business ideas for teens in 2024 (+ bonus quiz)*. https://www.shopify.com/blog/business-ideas-for-teens
- Social Media Examiner. (n.d.). *9 small business social media success stories*. https://www.socialmediaexaminer.com/9-small-business-social-media-success-stories/
- Square. (n.d.). *How to identify your target market*. https://squareup.com/us/en/the-bottom-line/series/marketing/how-to-identify-your-target-market)
- U.S. Chamber of Commerce. (n.d.). *5 financial planning tools for small businesses*. https://www.uschamber.com/co/run/finance/small-business-financial-planning-tools
- U.S. Census Bureau. (n.d.). *Statistics of U.S. Businesses (SUSB)*. https://www.census.gov/programs-surveys/susb.html
- U.S. Small Business Administration. (n.d.). *Register your business*. https://www.sba.gov/business-guide/launch-your-business/register-your-business
- U.S. Small Business Administration. (n.d.). *Small Business Economic Indicators*. https://www.sba.gov
- U.S. Securities and Exchange Commission. (n.d.). *Compound interest calculator*. Investor.gov. https://www.investor.gov/financial-tools-calculators/calculators/compound-interest-calculator
- WeWork. (n.d.). *Top 10 morning routines of highly successful people*. https://www.wework.com/ideas/professional-development/management-leadership/the-morning-routines-of-successful-people

Also by Chris Rosenberg

Book 2: Grow Money & Master Teen Finances

Made in United States
Troutdale, OR
12/22/2024

27182350R00080